Peyote Stit

Fresh projects to perfect your skills

Kalmbach
Media

Kalmbach Media
21027 Crossroads Circle
Waukesha, Wisconsin 53186
www.JewelryAndBeadingStore.com

Published in 2019
23 22 21 20 19   1 2 3 4 5

Manufactured in China

ISBN: 978-1-62700-680-4
EISBN: 978-1-62700-681-1

Editor: Erica Barse
Book Design: Lisa Bergman
Illustrator: Kellie Jaeger
Photographer: William Zuback

Library of Congress Control Number: 2018967291

Contents

Introduction

With just a needle and thread—and a handful of cylinder or seed beads—you can create the most gorgeous pieces of jewelry. Peyote stitch is one of the most popular stitches in *Bead&Button* magazine year after year, and it was an easy decision to address that desire for peyote projects with a collection of our favorite fresh designs using this versatile technique.

All the tried-and-true methods for peyote stitch are here: odd count, even count, flat, dimensional, and everything in between. With so many different looks and variations, you'll never get tired of the easy-but-endlessly fascinating stitch. The editors of *Bead&Button*, along with many talented contributors, have come up with so many ways to showcase peyote stitch via bracelets, earrings, necklaces, and pendants. This book even has a couple of ideas for using the latest, newest technique: peyote with a twist, or "Peytwist."

You can create bands, flowers, ropes, scenes, shapes, and so much more with adaptable, beautiful peyote stitch. It's easy to follow *Bead&Button's* clear illustrations, materials lists, and step-by-step instructions. For more help, you can also join our online community at facetjewelry.com. There you'll find additional patterns, colorways, and design variations for many of the projects in the book.

We hope you enjoy these pieces as you discover all that peyote has to offer.

Happy beading!

Erica Barse
Senior Editor, Kalmbach Books

Basics

Before you dive into peyote stitch,
take a moment to review a few basic
stitching necessities.

Materials

SEED BEADS

A huge variety of beads is available, but the beads most commonly used in
the projects in this book are seed beads. Seed beads come in packages, tubes,
and hanks. A standard hank (a looped bundle of beads strung on thread)
contains 12 20-in. (51 cm) strands, but vintage hanks are often much smaller.
Tubes and packages are usually measured in grams and vary in size.

Seed beads have been manufactured in many sizes ranging from the
largest, 5° (also called "E beads"), which are about 5 mm wide, to tiny size
20° or 22°, which aren't much larger than grains of sand. (The symbol $^{\circ}$
stands for "aught" or "zero." The greater the number of aughts, e.g., 22°, the
smaller the bead.) The most commonly available size in the widest range of
colors is 11°.

Most round seed beads are made in Japan and the Czech Republic. Czech
seed beads are slightly irregular and rounder than Japanese seed beads,
which are uniform in size and a bit squared off. Czech beads give a bumpier
surface when woven, but they reflect light at a wider range of angles. Japanese
seed beads produce a uniform surface and texture. Japanese and Czech seed
beads can be used together, but a Japanese seed bead is slightly larger than
the same size Czech seed bead.

Seed beads also come in sparkly cut versions. Japanese hex-cut or hex
beads are formed with six sides. 2- or 3-cut Czech beads are less regular.
Charlottes have an irregular facet cut on one side of the bead.

Japanese cylinder beads, otherwise known as Delicas (the Miyuki brand
name), Toho Treasures (the brand name of Toho), and Toho Aikos, are
extremely popular for peyote stitch projects. These beads are very regular
and have large holes, which are useful for stitches requiring multiple thread
passes. The beads fit together almost seamlessly, producing a smooth,
fabric-like surface.

note: Beads also come in a many, many other shapes as
well as multi-hole options, but for peyote stitch, round or
cylinder seed beads work best.

THREAD

Threads come in many sizes and strengths. Size (diameter or thickness) is
designated by a letter or number. OO and A/O are the thinnest; B, D, E, F,
and FF are subsequently thicker. Cord is measured on a number scale; 0 cor-
responds in thickness to D-size thread, 1 equals E, 2 equals F, and 3 equals
FF. Parallel filament nylon, such as Nymo or C-Lon, is made from
many thin nylon fibers that are extruded and heat-set to
form a single-ply thread. Parallel filament nylon is
durable and easy to thread, but it can be prone to
fraying and stretching. Plied nylon thread,
such as Silamide, is made from two or
more nylon threads that are extruded,
twisted together, and coated or

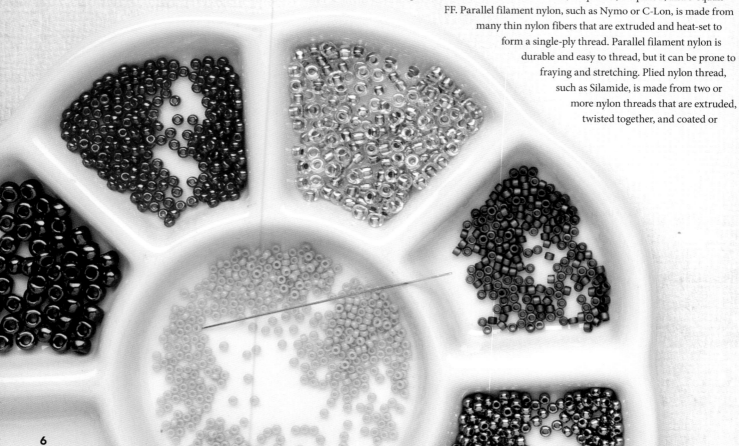

bonded for further strength, making them strong and durable. It is more resistant to fraying than parallel filament nylon, and some brands do not stretch.

Plied gel-spun polyethylene (GSP), such as Power Pro or DandyLine, is made from polyethylene fibers that have been spun into two or more threads that are braided together. It is almost unbreakable, it doesn't stretch, and it resists fraying. The thickness can make it difficult to make multiple passes through a bead.

Parallel filament GSP, such as Fireline, is a single-ply thread made from spun and bonded polyethylene fibers. It's extremely strong, it doesn't stretch, and it resists fraying. However, crystals may cut through parallel filament GSP, and smoke-colored varieties can leave a black residue on hands and beads.

NEEDLES

Beading needles are coded by size. The higher the number, the finer the beading needle. Unlike sewing needles, the eye of a beading needle is almost as narrow as its shaft. In addition to the size of the bead, the number of times you will pass through the bead also affects the needle size that you will use; if you will pass through a bead multiple times, you need to use a thinner needle.

Techniques

ADDING THREAD

To add a thread, sew into the beadwork several rows or rounds prior to the point where the last bead was added, leaving a short tail. Follow the thread path of the stitch, tying a few half-hitch knots (see "Half-hitch knot") between beads as you go, and exit where the last stitch ended. Trim the short tail.

CONDITIONING THREAD

Use beeswax or microcrystalline wax (not candle wax or paraffin) or Thread Heaven to condition nylon beading thread and Fireline. Wax smooths nylon fibers and adds tackiness that will stiffen your beadwork slightly. Thread Heaven adds a static charge that causes the thread to repel itself, so don't use it with doubled thread. Both conditioners help thread resist wear. To condition, stretch nylon thread to remove the curl (Fireline doesn't stretch). Lay the thread or Fireline on top of the conditioner, hold it in place with your thumb or finger, and pull the thread through the conditioner.

ENDING THREAD

To end a thread, sew back through the last few rows or rounds of beadwork, following the thread path of the stitch and tying two or three half-hitch knots (see "Half-hitch knot") between beads as you go. Sew through a few beads after the last knot, and trim the thread.

HALF-HITCH KNOT

Pass the needle under the thread bridge between two beads, and pull gently until a loop forms. Cross back over the thread between the beads, sew through the loop, and pull gently to draw the knot into the beadwork.

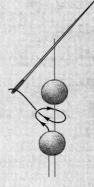

OVERHAND KNOT

Make a loop with the thread. Pull the tail through the loop, and tighten.

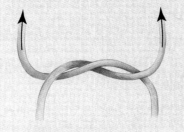

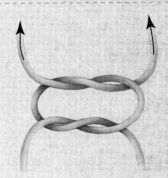

SQUARE KNOT

1) Cross one end of the thread over and under the other end. Pull both ends to tighten the first half of the knot.
2) Cross the first end of the thread over and under the other end. Pull both ends to tighten the knot.

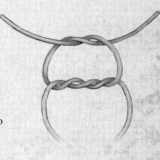

SURGEON'S KNOT

1) Cross one end of the thread over and under the other twice. Pull both ends to tighten the first half of the knot.
2) Cross the first end of the thread over and under the other end. Pull both ends to tighten the knot.

STOP BEAD

Use a stop bead to secure beads temporarily when you begin stitching. Choose a bead that is different from the beads in your project. Pick up the stop bead, leaving the desired-length tail. Sew through the stop bead again in the same direction, making sure you don't split the thread. If desired, sew through it one more time for added security.

Peyote stitch

The perfect technique for both flat bands and structural shapes, peyote stitch is wonderfully versatile. Regardless of the variation, all peyote techniques are based on the same basic thread path, which causes offset rows of beads to nestle together. If you're a beginner, start with the "Basic techniques." Try a few easy projects with these skills, and then move on to the more advanced techniques.

MATERIALS
samples
- assorted 15⁰–5⁰ seed beads
- Fireline, 6 lb. test, or nylon beading thread, size D
- beading needles, #12

TECHNIQUES TO KNOW
- basics: attaching a stop bead, square knot

Basic techniques

FLAT PEYOTE STITCH

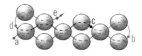

Flat even-count

The term "even-count peyote stitch" means that there are an even number of beads in each row.

1) Thread a needle on a comfortable length of thread, and attach a stop bead about 6 in. (15 cm) from the end. The stop bead isn't absolutely necessary, but it will prevent your beads from sliding off the thread, and it will also help you maintain good tension while you're stitching. Pick up an even number of beads **(figure, a–b)**. These beads will shift to form rows 1 and 2 as row 3 is added.

2) To begin row 3, pick up a bead, skip the last bead strung in the previous step, and sew back through the next bead in the opposite direction **(b–c)**. Position the new bead to sit next to the bead you skipped, so their holes are parallel. For each subsequent stitch in the row, pick up a bead, skip a bead in the previous step, and sew through the next bead, until your thread exits the first bead strung **(c–d)**. The beads added in this row stick out from the previous beads and are referred to as "up-beads."

3) For each stitch in subsequent rows, pick up a bead, and sew through the next up-bead in the previous row **(d–e)**.

tip Is your beadwork twisty and loose after working row 3, as in the top photo? Not to worry! Simply pull the working thread taut, pressing your thumbnail against the end bead to get the rows to straighten out.

tips for getting started!

If you're struggling with the first few rows, try one of these three methods:

- After stringing the beads for rows 1 and 2, pinch the beads between your thumb and forefinger. Pick up the first bead for row 3, skip the end bead, and sew back through the previous bead **(photo a)**. Continue holding the beads in place as you complete the row **(photo b)**.

- If the pinch method doesn't work for you, try passing a wire, pin, or needle through every other bead in the first strand **(photo c)**. This creates the peyote alignment, making it easier for you to see which beads to sew through in the next row.

- Another option is to use a Quick Start Peyote card. These durable, laminated cards have openings to hold the beads in row 1, turning them into up-beads from the start **(photo d)**. This makes it a cinch to add subsequent rows. Get them at www.quick-startpeyote.com.

a

b

c

d

Flat odd-count

Flat odd-count peyote stitch has an odd number of beads in every other row. It is worked with the same thread path as even-count peyote, except for the turn after odd-numbered rows, where the last bead of the row can't be attached in the usual way because there is no up-bead to sew through. Begin an odd-count piece as follows:

1) Pick up an odd number of beads. Work row 3 as in even-count peyote, stopping before adding the last bead.

2) Work a figure-8 turn at the end of row 3: Sew through the first bead picked up in step 1 (bead #1). Pick up the last bead of the odd-numbered row (bead #8), and sew through beads #2, #3, #7, #2, #1, and #8.

3) Work row 4 as in even-count peyote, and then work row 5, stopping before adding the last bead.

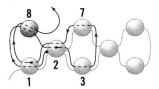

4) In this and all subsequent odd-numbered rows, work the following turn: Pick up the last bead of the row, and then sew under the edge thread bridge immediately below. Sew back through the last bead added to begin the next row.

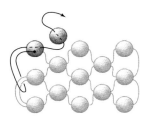

ZIPPING UP OR JOINING

To join two sections of a peyote piece invisibly, match up the two sections so the end rows fit together like puzzle pieces. If the end rows don't fit together, add or remove one row of peyote from either section. Then "zip up" the sections by zigzagging through the up-beads on both ends.

tip Zigzag back through the beadwork to complete the join, making sure you connect the end beads on each edge.

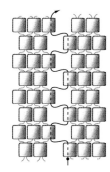

TWO-DROP PEYOTE STITCH

Work two-drop peyote stitch the same way as basic flat peyote, but treat pairs of beads as if they were single beads.

1) To work in even-count two-drop peyote, pick up an even number of beads that is divisible by four. To work in odd-count two-drop peyote, pick up an even number of beads that is not divisible by four. Remember, these beads will shift to form rows 1 and 2 as row 3 is added.

2) To begin row 3, pick up two beads, skip two beads added in step 1, and sew back through the next two beads. Repeat this stitch across the row.

3) If you are working in even-count two-drop peyote, you will not need to do anything special to turn and begin subsequent rows. If you are working in odd-count two-drop peyote, modify the turns as in steps 2 and 4 of "Flat odd-count peyote."

tip Yes, you can do three-drop peyote or four-drop or five-drop or... you get the picture. If you want your piece to be even-count, make sure the total number of beads you pick up for the first two rows is divisible by two and the number of beads you want in each "drop." You can also mix counts in a piece, so you might have a row that has a stitch with one bead, a stitch with two beads, and a stitch with three beads. See what kinds of interesting patterns and textures you can create just by playing around with bead counts!

TUBULAR PEYOTE STITCH

Tubular peyote stitch follows the same stitching pattern as basic flat peyote, but instead of sewing back and forth, you work in rounds to form a tube.

Tubular even-count

1) Pick up an even number of beads to equal the desired circumference. Tie the beads into a ring with a square knot, leaving some slack between the beads, and sew through the first bead after the knot (**figure, a–b**). These beads will shift to form rounds 1 and 2 as round 3 is added.

2) Put the ring over a form if desired. To begin round 3, pick up a bead, skip the next bead in the ring, and sew through the following bead (**b–c**). Repeat this stitch to complete the round (**c–d**), and "step up" by sewing through the first up-bead added in this round (**d–e**). Stepping up positions your thread to begin the next round.

3) To work subsequent rounds, pick up a bead, and sew through the next up-bead in the previous round. Repeat this stitch to complete the round, and step up.

4) Repeat step 3 to the desired length.

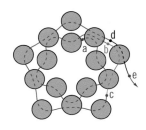

Tubular odd-count

In odd-count tubular peyote, you don't need to step up; the beads will automatically form a continuous spiral.

1) Pick up an odd number of beads, tie them into a ring with a square knot, and sew through the first bead again **(figure, a–b)**. These beads will shift to form rounds 1 and 2 as round 3 is added.

2) Work round 3 in tubular peyote stitch until you sew through the bead prior to the first bead in the ring **(b–c)**. Pick up a bead, and sew through the next up-bead **(c–d)**.

3) For subsequent rounds, continue working in tubular peyote, always sewing through the next up-bead.

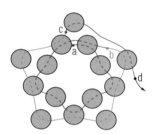

CIRCULAR PEYOTE STITCH

Circular peyote stitch is worked in rounds like tubular peyote, but the rounds stay flat and radiate outward from the center as a result of incorporating increase stitches or larger beads in subsequent rounds.

tip

It's easy to make striped patterns in tubular peyote!

- To begin a tube with spiral stripes, alternate pairs of beads in each of two colors in the original ring. For subsequent rounds, pick up a bead of the opposite color as the bead directly below it for each stitch in the round.

- For vertical stripes, begin with a ring of beads that alternates color with every other bead. For subsequent rounds, pick up a bead of the same color as the bead directly below it for each stitch in the round.

- For horizontal stripes, start with a ring of beads in a single color. Work two or more rounds in the same color depending on the desired width of the stripe, and then switch to a second color for the next two or more rounds. Alternate colors for the desired length.

- Combine these techniques to create a tube of all three stripes (right).

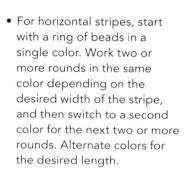

Shaping techniques

INCREASING AND DECREASING AT EDGES

Even-count increase

To increase one row along the edge when working in flat even-count peyote, pick up two beads, and sew through them again. Continue in the opposite direction to stitch the new row.

Even-count decrease

To decrease one row along the edge when working in flat even-count peyote, sew under the nearest thread bridge along the edge, and sew back through the last two beads you just sewed through.

Odd-count increase

To increase one row along the edge when working in flat odd-count peyote, pick up the final bead for the row you're finishing, and sew through the adjacent bead and the bead just added. Pick up two beads, and sew back through the first bead added.

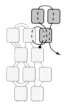

Odd-count decrease

To decrease one row along the edge when working in flat odd-count peyote, omit the final stitch in the row. Pick up a bead to begin the next row, and sew back through the last up-bead in the previous row.

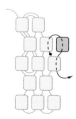

DECREASING AND INCREASING WITHIN A PIECE

Decreasing

1) At the point of decrease, sew through two up-beads in the previous row.

2) In the next row, when you reach the two-bead space, pick up one bead.

3) Continue working in regular peyote stitch.

Increasing

1) At the point of increase, pick up two beads instead of one. Sew through the next bead.

2) When you reach the two beads in the next row, sew through the first bead, pick up a bead, and sew through the second bead. This is sometimes referred to as "splitting the increase."

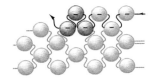

3) Continue working in regular peyote stitch.

tip Not all beads of any given type are shaped the same, and you can use that to your advantage when increasing and decreasing. For instance, when you add two beads for an increase, choose two narrow beads. In the next row when you split the increase, use another narrow bead. In the following row, go back to using standard size beads. Likewise, when decreasing, pick up a wide bead when you are going over the point of decrease. In the following rows, you can use regular size beads.

Advanced techniques

FAST PEYOTE

In fast peyote, you pick up all the beads for two rows or rounds at a time instead of repeatedly picking up one bead and stitching it in place. Be sure you are comfortable with the regular peyote technique before trying fast peyote so that you understand the mechanics of the stitch. We learned this technique from Dona Anderson, who got it from a Native American friend.

Flat even-count

1) Pick up an even number of beads to form rows 1 and 2. Work in flat even-count peyote stitch until you have a total of four rows.

2) Pick up the same number of beads you started with in step 1 (that is, enough beads for two rows). Drape them across the beadwork, and sew through the end up-bead in the previous row, going in the opposite direction.

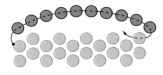

3) Skip the last bead picked up in step 2, sew through the next one, and continue through the next up-bead in the previous row (a–b). Repeat this stitch across the row, zigzagging through every other bead picked up in step 2 and the up-beads in the previous row (b–c).

4) Repeat steps 2 and 3 for the desired length.

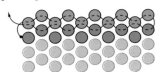

Flat odd-count

1) Pick up an odd number of beads to form rows 1 and 2. Work in flat odd-count peyote stitch until you have a total of four rows.

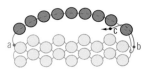

2) Exiting an edge down-bead, pick up the same number of beads you picked up to begin step 1. Drape them across the beadwork, and sew under the thread bridge on the opposite edge (a–b). Sew through the last bead picked up, going in the opposite direction (b–c).

3) Sew through the next up-bead in the previous row, skip the next bead in the group you picked up in step 2, and sew through the following bead (a–b). Repeat this stitch across the row, zigzagging through every other bead in the new group and the up-beads in the previous row. Exit the first bead picked up in step 2 (b–c).

4) Repeat steps 2 and 3 for the desired length.

tip While fast peyote does hasten your stitching, you'll get bogged down if you pick up the wrong beads, so always double check that you've got the right beads on your needle before stitching them in place.

MORE FAST PEYOTE
Tubular even-count

1) Pick up an even number of beads, tie them into a ring with a square knot, and sew through the first bead again.

2) Work in tubular even-count peyote stitch until you have a total of four rounds.

3) Pick up the same number of beads you picked up in step 1, and sew through the first bead just picked up.

4) Sew through the next up-bead in the previous round.

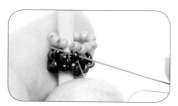

Skip the next bead in the group you picked up in step 3, and sew through the following bead.

Repeat this stitch to complete the round, and step up through the first two beads picked up in this round.

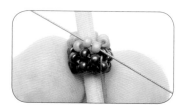

5) Repeat steps 3 and 4 for the desired length.

Tubular odd-count

1) Pick up an odd number of beads, tie them into a ring with a square knot, and sew through the first bead again.

2) Work in tubular odd-count peyote stitch until you have a total of four rounds.

3) Pick up the same number of beads you picked up in step 1, and sew through the first bead again.

4) Sew through the next up-bead in the previous round, skip the next bead in the group you picked up in step 3, and sew through the following bead. Repeat this stitch until you've sewn through the last bead picked up in step 3. You do not need to step up.

5) Repeat steps 3 and 4 for the desired length.

tip For straight and precise lines and edges, be sure to cull your beads as you work, setting aside any that are too wide, narrow, or misshapen.

tip When your thread gets short, always add a new thread before ending the old one. Work a few rows or rounds with the new thread, and then end the old thread in the beadwork. This will ensure that you resume stitching in the right direction.

DIAGONAL PEYOTE

Diagonal peyote is a result of working flat peyote with an increase at one edge and a decrease at the other edge with every pair of rows.

1) To create a diagonal band, work three rows of flat even-count peyote stitch (**a–b**).

2) Work an increase: Pick up three beads, and sew back through the first bead just picked up (**b–c**). Working in the other direction, continue in peyote stitch, stopping short of the final stitch in the row (**c–d**).

3) Work a decrease: Pick up a bead, and sew back through the last up-bead in the previous row (**d–e**). Continue in peyote to complete the row (**e–f**).

4) Repeat steps 2 and 3 (**f–g**) to the desired length, always working an increase along one edge and a decrease along the other edge.

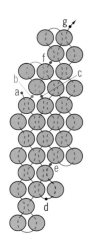

STITCH IN THE DITCH

The "stitch in the ditch" technique is done on top of an existing layer of peyote. Exit the beadwork as directed in the project instructions. Pick up a bead, and sew through the next bead in the same row. Repeat across the row or as directed.

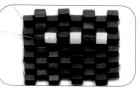

PEYOTE TOGGLE CLASPS

The following instructions make a ¾-in. (1.9 cm) toggle clasp. Adjust bead counts if you want a larger clasp.

To make a toggle ring: On 1 yd. (.9 m) of thread, pick up 36–40 15º seed beads, and tie them into a ring with a square knot, leaving a 12-in. (30 cm) tail. Work a round of even-count tubular peyote stitch using 15ºs, and then work two rounds with 11º seed or cylinder beads. Using the tail, work a round using 11ºs, and then zip up the two edge rounds to form a ring.

To make a toggle bar: On 1 yd. (.9 m) of thread, pick up 14–16 11º or 15º seed beads, leaving a 6-in. (15 cm) tail. Work a total of 10–14 rows of flat even- or odd-count peyote, roll the strip into a tube, and zip up the end rows.

CELLINI SPIRAL

The Cellini spiral was originated by seed bead masters Virginia Blakelock and Carol Perrenoud, who developed the tubular variation and named it after Benvenuto Cellini, a 16th-century Italian sculptor known for his Rococo architectural columns. Eventually, the flat version emerged, and both techniques are equally beautiful.

tip In peyote stitch, the beads nestle together, so to figure out how many rows or rounds you've stitched, identify a diagonal line of beads, and count how many there are in the diagonal line.

Flat Cellini spiral

1) Pick up two color A 15º seed beads, two color B 15º seed beads, two As, two color C 11º cylinder beads, and two color D 11º seed beads **(figure, a–b)**. These beads will shift to form rows 1 and 2 as row 3 is added.

2) Work in flat even-count peyote stitch, picking up the following beads, one per stitch:

Row 3: C, D, C, A, B **(b–c)**.
Row 4: B, A, C, D, C **(c–d)**.
Row 5: A, C, D, C, A **(d–e)**.
Row 6: A, C, D, C, A **(e–f)**.
Row 7: B, A, C, D, C **(f–g)**.
Row 8: C, D, C, A, B **(g–h)**.
Row 9: A, B, A, C, D **(h–i)**.
Row 10: D, C, A, B, A **(i–j)**.
Row 11: C, A, B, A, C **(j–k)**.

3) Rows 12–20: Work rows 11–3 in reverse **(k–l)**.

4) Work three more rows to complete the pattern:

Row 21: A, B, A, C, D **(l–m)**.
Row 22: D, C, A, B, A **(m–n)**.
Row 23: C, A, B, A, C **(n–o)**.

5) Repeat steps 3 and 4 until you reach the desired length.

Tubular Cellini spiral

1) Pick up two color A 15º seed beads, two color B 15º seed beads, two color C 11º cylinder beads, two color D 11º seed beads, two color E 8º seed beads, two Ds, and two Cs. Tie the beads into a ring with a square knot, and sew through the first two As again **(figure 1, a–b)**. These beads will shift to form rounds 1 and 2 as round 3 is added.

2) Work round 3 in tubular peyote stitch, picking up the following beads, one per stitch: A, B, C, D, E, D, C. Step up through the first A in the new round **(b–c)**.

3) Repeat step 2 **(figure 2)** to the desired length.

tip To enhance the sculptural aspect of tubular Cellini spiral, gently squeeze the opening of the beadwork as you stitch. This will help you maintain the tension and prevent gaps between beads of different sizes.

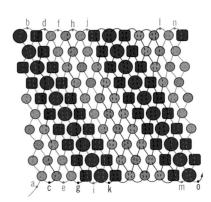

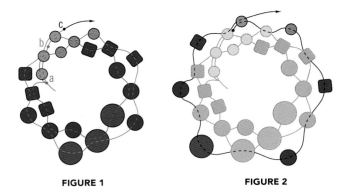

FIGURE 1　　　**FIGURE 2**

tip to get a grip Literally. Picking up your beadwork and holding it while you stitch can greatly improve your stitching tension. Hold both the working thread and the bead you just added to prevent the stitch from loosening up as you add the next bead. Let go of the previous stitch only once the next stitch is completed, and then only to move your grasp to the next stitch.

DUTCH SPIRAL

Similar to tubular Cellini spiral, Dutch spiral is a sculptural variant of tubular peyote. The distinguishing characteristic is a loose "bridge" of beads that spans one section of the beadwork, and it tends to be more flexible than tubular Cellini spiral. Just about any types of seed beads can be used in Dutch spiral. The beads used in the sample shown here are:

As – 11º hex-cut beads
Bs – 10º seed beads
Cs – 8º seed beads
Ds – 5º triangle beads
Es – 6º seed beads
Fs – 11º seed beads

1) Pick up an A, two Bs, two Cs, two Ds, two Es, and seven Fs. Tie the beads into a ring with a square knot, and sew through the A again **(figure 1)**.

2) Work a round of tubular peyote, picking up the following beads, one per stitch: A, B, C, D **(figure 2, a–b)**. Pick up an E and seven Fs, and sew through the A picked up at the start of the round **(b–c)**.

3) Repeat step 2 for the desired length. Alternatively, you can vary the number of Fs picked up to create a piece with a graduated spiral.

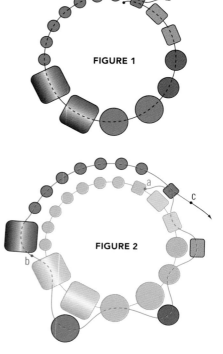

FIGURE 1

FIGURE 2

Peyote bezels

If you want to capture round or shaped stones in beaded bezels, look no further. These instructions will show you how to make perfect peyote stitch bezels every time.

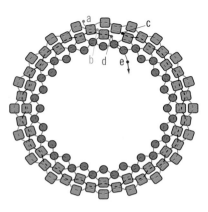

FIGURE 1

ROUND BEZELS

1) On 1 yd. (.9 m) of thread, pick up enough 11° cylinder beads to fit around the circumference of a rivoli or stone. See the chart below for the approximate number of cylinders to start with. Center the beads on the thread, and sew through the first cylinder again to form a ring (**figure 1, a–b**).

2) Pick up a cylinder, skip the next cylinder in the ring, and sew through the following cylinder (**b–c**). Continue working in tubular peyote stitch to complete the round, and step up through the first cylinder added (**c–d**).

3) Work the next two rounds in tubular peyote using 15° seed beads (**d–e**). Keep the tension tight to decrease the size of the ring.

BEZELING RIVOLIS: How many cylinders do I pick up?

It can be challenging to guess how many cylinders to pick up in the initial bezel ring. Two important tips: The initial ring should always have an even number of beads, and it should fit around the widest part of your stone. Though these counts may vary slightly depending upon your beads and stitching tension, this is a good place to start when bezeling.

Size of rivoli/stone	Number of cylinders
12 mm	30
14 mm	36
16 mm	40
18 mm	46
22 x 30 mm	64

4) Position the rivoli or stone in the bezel cup. Using the other thread, work one round of tubular peyote along the other edge using cylinder beads, and two rounds using 15°s (**figure 2**).

SQUARE RIVOLI (12 MM)

1) On a comfortable length of thread, pick up a repeating pattern of five cylinders and four 15°s four times, and sew through the first cylinder again (**figure 3, a–b**), leaving a 12-in. (30 cm) tail.

2) Work two stitches in tubular peyote using cylinders (**b–c**). Pick up a 15°, skip the first 15° in the ring, and sew through the next two 15°s (**c–d**). Work one stitch with a 15° (**d–e**). Repeat these stitches three times to complete the round, and step up to start the next round (**e–f**).

3) Work a round of tubular peyote, picking up one 15° in each stitch, and treating the two 15°s at each corner as one bead (**f–g**).

4) Work a peyote stitch, and sew through the next two 15°s without picking up a new 15° (**g–h**). Pick up a 15°, and sew through the next up-15°. Continue around, decreasing at the remaining corners the same way (**h–i**).

5) Place the rivoli in the bezel, and, using the tail thread, sew through the next 15° in the first round (**figure 4, a–b**).

6) Pick up two 15°s, skip two 15°s, and sew through the next 15°. Work three peyote stitches using cylinders (**b–c**). Repeat around, and step up (**c–d**).

7) Work a round of tubular peyote using 15°s, sewing through the two 15°s at each corner as if they were a single bead, and step up (**d–e**). Work a second round of 15°s to complete the bezel, treating the two-bead stitches as a single bead (**e–f**).

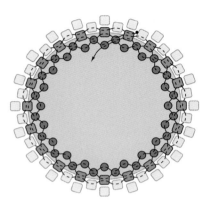

FIGURE 2

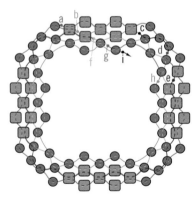

FIGURE 3

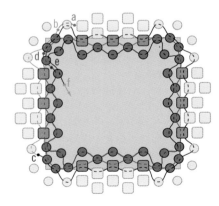

FIGURE 4

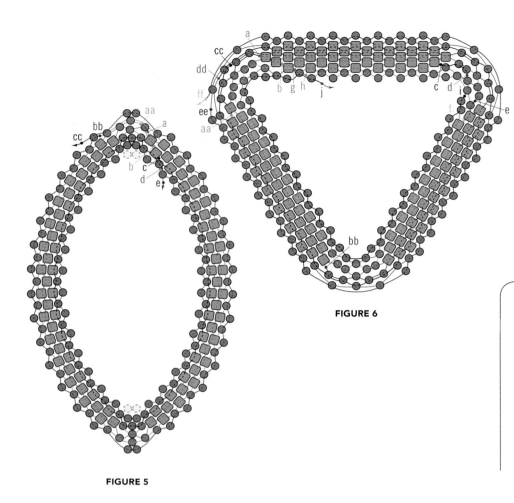

FIGURE 6

FIGURE 5

materials
each bezel

- crystal rivoli or shaped stone
- 1–2 g 11º cylinder beads
- 1 g 15º seed beads
- Fireline, 6 lb. test, or nylon beading thread, size D
- beading needles, #12

techniques to know

- peyote stitch: tubular

NAVETTE STONE (32 X 17 MM)

1) On a comfortable length of thread, pick up 29 cylinders and three 15ºs twice, and sew through the first cylinder again to form a ring, leaving an 18-in. (46 cm) tail **(figure 5, a–b)**.

2) Work a round of tubular peyote, picking up cylinders where you skip cylinders and 15ºs where you skip 15ºs **(b–c)**.

3) Work a round of peyote picking up a 15º for each stitch **(c–d)**.

4) Work a round of peyote, picking up one 15º for each stitch on the long sides (where the cylinders sit). Skip the center bead in each corner, picking up two 15ºs to span the distance, instead of one **(d–e)**.

5) Place the stone in the bezel so the back is nestled in the beads. If the hold is not secure, you may want to add two 15ºs to each corner.

6) Using the tail thread, sew through the next 15º **(a–aa)**, and work a round of peyote, picking up a 15º in each stitch. Sew through three 15ºs to step up **(aa–bb)**.

7) Work the final round as you did in step 4 **(bb–cc)**.

TRIANGULAR STONE (23 MM)

1) On a comfortable length of thread, pick up a repeating pattern of 17 cylinders and five 15ºs three times, leaving an 18-in. (46 cm) tail. Sew through the first two cylinders again to form a ring **(figure 6, a–b)**.

2) Work seven peyote stitches using cylinders **(b–c)**, pick up a 15º, and sew through the next two 15ºs **(c–d)**. Pick up a 15º, skip the next 15º in the ring, and sew through the next two 15ºs **(d–e)**. Pick up a 15º skip the next cylinder, and sew through the following cylinder **(e–f)**. Repeat around, and step up **(f–g)**.

3) Work a round of tubular peyote, picking up one 15º for each stitch **(g–h)**.

4) Work seven peyote stitches, picking up one 15º in each stitch, and then sew through the next 15º without adding a bead **(h–i)**. Continue around in tubular peyote, decreasing at each corner **(i–j)**.

5) Fit the stone in the bezel, and, using the tail thread, pick up two 15ºs, sew through the next 15º, pick up two 15ºs, skip two 15ºs, and sew through the next up-cylinder **(a–aa)**. Work eight peyote stitches using cylinders **(aa–bb)**. Repeat around the stone, then step up **(bb–cc)**.

6) Work a round of peyote using the same stitch pattern as in step 2: a 15º, a 15º, seven cylinders, a 15º. Repeat around, and step up **(cc–dd)**.

7) Work a round of tubular peyote, picking up one 15º in each stitch, and step up **(dd–ee)**.

8) Work a round of tubular peyote using 15ºs and decreasing in each corner, as in step 4 **(ee–ff)**.

Making peyote shapes

techniques by
Julia Gerlach

Basic geometric shapes are fun and easy to make with beads. Get started with a peyote triangle and then use the same principle to make squares, pentagons, and hexagons. After you learn to make these basic flat shapes, combine them for three-dimensional effects.

FLAT TRIANGLE

1) The basic concept behind this technique is that you will always start each shape with a ring of beads that is equal to the number of sides the shape will have. A triangle obviously has three sides, so start by picking up three beads on about 18 in. (46 cm) of thread.

Leaving a 6-in. (15 cm) tail, sew through all the beads again to form a ring, and then sew through the first bead once more. The working thread and tail will be exiting opposite sides of the same bead. This is round 1.

2) Work in rounds as follows. The diagrams show each round in a different color for clarity.
Round 2: Pick up two seed beads, and sew through the next bead in the ring **(figure 1, a–b)**. Repeat this stitch twice, and step up through the first bead added in this round **(b–c)**.
Round 3: Pick up two beads, and sew down through the next bead

in the previous round **(c–d)**. The two new beads will stack on top of the previous pair. Work one peyote stitch by picking up a bead, and sewing up through the first bead in the next pair **(d–e)**. Repeat these two stitches twice to complete the round, and step up **(e–f)**.
The two-bead columns are worked in herringbone and will form the corners. The single-bead peyote stitches will form the sides.
Rounds 4 and beyond: Work as in round 2, but for each round, work one more peyote stitch on each side than in the previous round **(f–g)**.
Final round: When your triangle is the desired size, work a final round,

picking up three beads instead of two at each corner **(g–h)**. End the tail but not the working thread.

3D TRIANGLE

If you want to go 3D, you'll need to make a total of four triangles and then zip them together at the edges. Because the edges of the triangles need to interlock, they can't be identical, so you'll need to work a joining round on just one edge of each join.
1) To begin, work another round on one triangle, but don't add any beads at the corners **(figure 2)**.
2) Align the other triangles so the edge up-beads nestle together,

materials
basic geometric shapes

- **1 g** 8º or 11º cylinder or seed beads
- beading needle, #11
- WildFire or Fireline, 6 lb. test, or nylon beading thread, size D

basics

- peyote stitch: flat, even-count; flat, odd-count; zipping up or joining
- herringbone stitch
- ending and adding thread

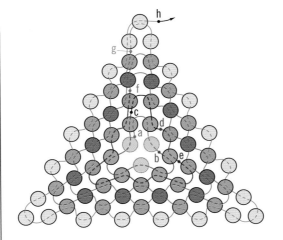

FIGURE 1

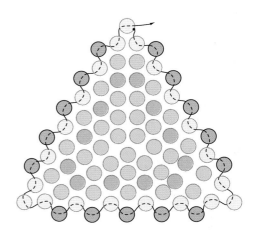

FIGURE 2

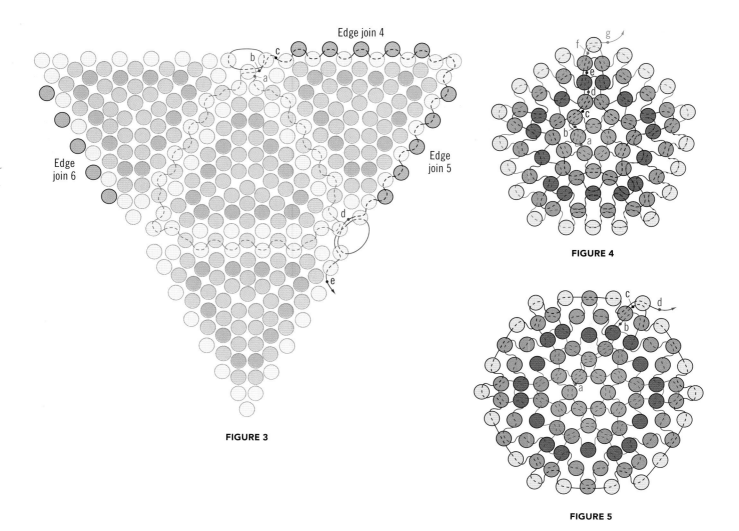

FIGURE 3

FIGURE 4

FIGURE 5

and then zip up the edges, sewing through the existing corner beads on the center triangle (**figure 3, a–b**). These are the first three edge joins. You will need to do three more joins to complete the triangle.

3) Sew through the three adjacent corner beads (**b–c**).

4) Add another round on the remaining two edges on one of the outer triangles (**c–d**), and then sew through the nearest three corner beads to bring them together. The triangle shape will be apparent now but three edges remain unjoined.

5) Zip up the two edges on the adjacent side (labeled Edge join 4 in **figure 3**), sew through the corner beads, and then zip up the other edge that already has the joining beads added (Edge join 5).

6) Sew through the beadwork to the remaining unjoined edge.

Add joining beads to one side, and then zip up the edge and sew through the remaining unjoined corner beads to complete the triangle (Edge join 6). End any remaining threads.

PENTAGON

1) On 18 in. (46 cm) of thread, begin with a ring of five seed beads (**figure 4, a–b**).

2) Work in rounds as follows:
Round 2: Work a round of peyote with one bead per stitch (**b–c**).
Round 3: Work five corner stitches with two beads per stitch (**c–d**).
Round 4: Work a round that alternates between a two-bead corner stitch and a one-bead side stitch (**d–e**).
Round 5: Work an alternating pattern of a corner stitch and two side stitches five times (**e–f**).

Round 6: Work an alternating pattern of a corner stitch and three side stitches, but pick up only one bead at each corner (**f–g**). You can make a 3D pentagon, known as a dodecahedron, but you'll need 12 flat pentagons and you may need to fill your shape to give it support.

SQUARE

To make a square, start with a ring of four beads, and work in rounds:
Round 2: Work a round of peyote with one bead per stitch.
Round 3: Work four corner stitches with two beads per stitch.
Rounds 4 and beyond: Alternate between corners and sides for the desired number of rounds.
To make a cube, make six flat squares, and join them together at the edges, as in the 3D triangle.

HEXAGON

1) Work as in rounds 1–4 of the pentagon, but begin with six beads instead of five (**figure 5 a–b**).

2) Work in rounds as follows:
Round 5: Alternate a corner stitch and a three-bead side stitch, skipping the side bead in the previous round (**b–c**).

Round 6: Alternate a one-bead corner stitch and two side stitches, sewing through the center bead of each three-bead stitch in the previous round (**c–d**). You can't make a 3D shape with just hexagons. However, if you're up for a challenge, you can use a combination of shapes like hexagons and squares to make a make a 3D form, such as a truncated octahedron.

Right-angle peyote

An abundance of design possibilities spring from a simple seed bead component. Learn the basic structure, and explore several options for creating beautiful bracelets.

techniques by
Antonio Calles

This technique is called "right-angle peyote" because it has elements of both right-angle weave and peyote stitch. Altering the color placement and arrangement of the components creates a wide range of different looks.

BASIC COMPONENT

Instructions for the basic component will be shown in a single color so you can learn the technique without worrying about what color to pick up. Colors will be introduced in the project patterns.

1) On a comfortable length of thread, pick up four 11º seed beads, leaving a 6-in. (15 cm) tail. Sew through the beads again to form a tight ring.

2) Pick up an 11º, and sew through the next 11º in the ring. Repeat three times, and step up through the first 11º added in this round **(figure 1)**.

3) Pick up two 11ºs, and sew through the next 11º in the previous round. Repeat three times, and step up through the first 11º added in this round **(figure 2)**.

4) Pick up an 11º, and sew through the next 11º in the previous round. This is a corner stitch. Pick up an 11º, and sew through the next 11º.

This is a side stitch. Repeat the two stitches three times to complete the round, and step up through the first 11º added in this round **(figure 3)**.

note In the projects that follow, some (or all) of the side 11ºs added in step 4 will occasionally be omitted. To omit side beads, simply sew through a bead in the previous row where you would normally add a bead. Figure 4 shows adding all four corners and skipping three of the side beads.

SUBSEQUENT COMPONENTS

1) To begin the next component, pick up three 11ºs. Sew through the 11º your thread exited at the start of this step. Retrace the thread path to secure the ring, and exit the second new 11º **(figure 5)**. This is a right-angle weave stitch.

2) Work another right-angle weave (RAW) stitch with three 11ºs, exiting the same 11º **(figure 6)**.

FIGURE 1

FIGURE 2

FIGURE 3

FIGURE 4

FIGURE 5

FIGURE 6

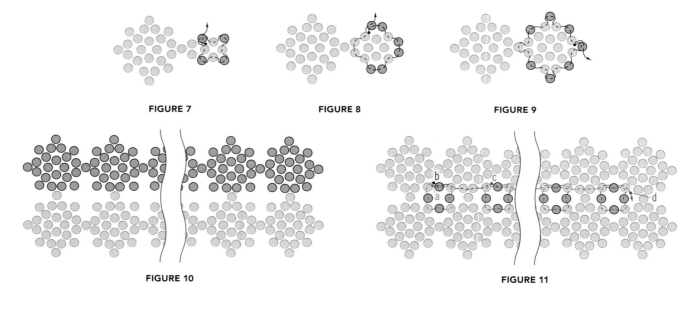

FIGURE 7 FIGURE 8 FIGURE 9

FIGURE 10 FIGURE 11

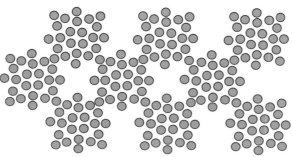

FIGURE 12

3) Repeat step 2 of "Basic component" to add four 11ºs (**figure 7**). Repeat step 3 of "Basic component," but add only three pairs of 11ºs. Instead of adding the fourth pair, sew through the adjacent pair of 11ºs that were added in the first stitch of this component (**figure 8**). Repeat step 4 of "Basic component" to add three corner and four side beads (**figure 9**).

4) Continue adding components to reach the desired length.

SUBSEQUENT ROWS

To add another parallel row of components, begin a new component with a new thread, as in steps 1–3 of "Basic component." Work as in step 4 to add four side beads and three corner beads, sewing through the appropriate corner bead on the previous row. Exit the adjacent cor-

ner bead of the new component, and work as in "Subsequent components" to the desired length, being sure to attach each new component to the previous row (**figure 10**).

FILLING THE GAPS

When you connect two rows of components, the result will be somewhat airy due to gaps at the intersections between the components. Filling those gaps can give your beadwork an entirely different look. To fill the gaps, sew through the beadwork to exit a side bead where four components come together. Pick up an 11º, and sew through the corresponding side bead on the adjacent component. Repeat three times (**figure 11, a–b**), and then sew through the four new beads added to cinch them together (not shown in the

figure for clarity). Sew through the beadwork to exit the corresponding side bead in the next gap (**b–c**). Repeat to fill all the gaps (**c–d**).

DIAGONAL ROWS

Working short diagonal rows instead of long parallel rows will also create a different look. The "Lacy bracelet" (p. 22) is worked in diagonal rows of three components. It's a bit more time consuming to work diagonally because you have to keep switching directions. Figure 12 gives a basic idea of how the diagonal rows should be oriented.

PARTIAL COMPONENTS

Partial components can also be used for a creative edging, as in the "Lacy bracelet."

materials
sample bracelets

- **3–4 g** 11º seed beads in each of **3** colors, A, B, C
- nylon beading thread, size D
- beading needles, #11

Find Word charts and blank patterns for the bracelets at

FacetJewelry.com/ resourceguide

basics

- peyote stitch: circular
- right-angle weave
- ending and adding thread

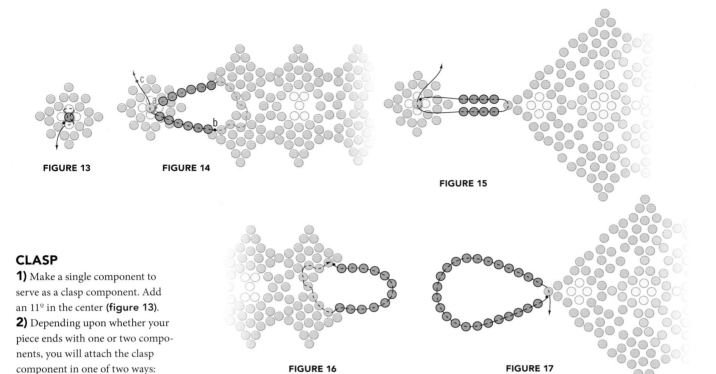

FIGURE 13

FIGURE 14

FIGURE 15

FIGURE 16

FIGURE 17

CLASP

1) Make a single component to serve as a clasp component. Add an 11º in the center (**figure 13**).

2) Depending upon whether your piece ends with one or two components, you will attach the clasp component in one of two ways:

Double connection: Exiting the center 11º, pick up six 11ºs, and sew through the end two components as shown (**figure 14, a–b**). Pick up six 11ºs, and sew through the center 11º on the clasp component (**b–c**). Retrace the thread path through the connection a few times, and end the thread.

Single connection: Exiting the center 11º, pick up four 11ºs, and sew through the 11º at the tip of the end component. Pick up four 11ºs, and sew through the center 11º on the clasp component (**figure 15**). Retrace the thread path through the connection a few times, and end the thread.

3) At the other end of the bracelet, make a loop in one of two ways:

Double connection: Exit a bead next to the tip bead on an end component. Pick up 12 11ºs, and sew through the corresponding 11º on the adjacent component. Sew through the beadwork (**figure 16**),

retrace the thread path through the loop, and end the thread.

Single connection: Exit the tip bead of the end component, pick up 24 11ºs, and sew through the tip bead again (**figure 17**). Retrace the thread path a few times, and end the thread.

NARROW BRACELET

This bracelet consists of two connected strips of basic components with the intersections filled. Refer to **figure 18** to make this bracelet, noting that the row 1 beads are outlined in black, row 2 beads are outlined in green, and the intersection beads are outlined in red.

1) On a comfortable length of thread, work row 1, placing colors A, B, and C 11ºs as indicated. Each end component is all color A and all the remaining components should include all three colors. Note that no side beads are added along the color A edge. Only the color B/C edge should have side beads. A 7½-in. (19.1 cm) bracelet will need 16 A/B/C components.

2) Make a second strip to match the first, but connect it to the first strip as you work, sewing through existing corner beads instead of adding new ones.

3) Fill the intersections with As and Bs as indicated by the beads outlined in red.

4) Make a clasp component, attach it with a double connection, and make a double connection loop.

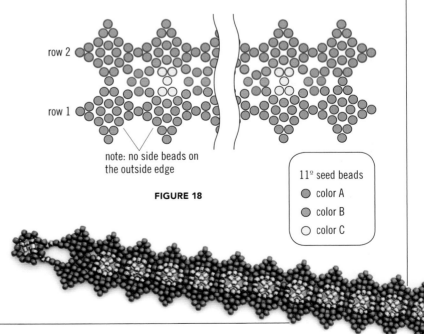

row 2

row 1

note: no side beads on the outside edge

FIGURE 18

11º seed beads
- ● color A
- ● color B
- ○ color C

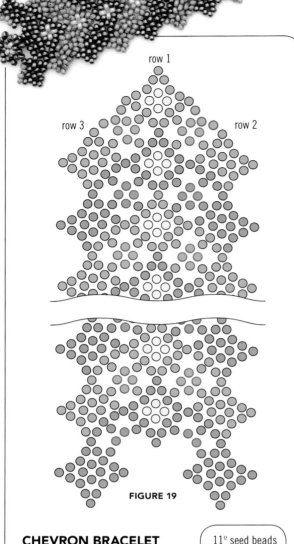

row 1

row 3   row 2

FIGURE 19

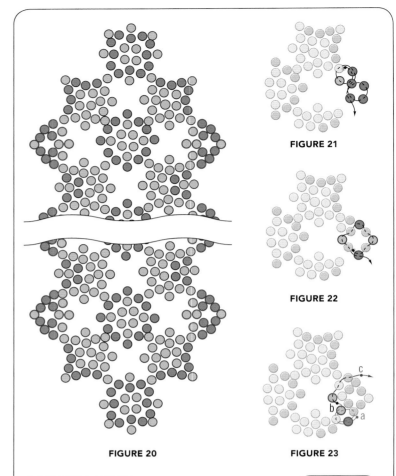

FIGURE 21

FIGURE 22

c

b   a

FIGURE 20   **FIGURE 23**

CHEVRON BRACELET

11° seed beads
○ color A
◑ color B
○ color C

The Chevron bracelet is three rows wide and has the intersections filled. Refer to **figure 19** to make this bracelet, noting that the intersection beads are outlined in red.

1) On a comfortable length of thread, work row 1, placing colors A, B, and C as indicated. Note that except for the starting component, which has only two side beads, all the rest of the components in row 1 require four side beads. In our 7½-in. (19.1 cm) bracelet, row 1 has 18 components.

2) Begin row 2 with a new component, and attach it to the second component in row 1. Note that the outer edge will not need side beads. Row 2 should extend past row 1 by one component.

3) Work row 3 as a mirror image of row 2, connecting it on the other side of row 1.

4) Fill the intersections with As and Bs as indicated by the beads outlined in red.

5) At the starting end, you will need to add a few fill-in beads to create a smooth edge. The beads are outlined in green.

6) Make a clasp component, attach it with a single connection, and make a single connection loop.

LACY BRACELET

The Lacy bracelet is built on diagonal rows of three components each (except at the ends). Partial components embellish the outer edges. No intersections are filled, contributing to the lacy appearance. Refer to **figure 20** to make this bracelet, noting that the edge beads (outlined in purple) are partial components. See step 3 to learn how to add these.

1) On a comfortable length of thread, work the end center component, placing colors A, B, and C as indicated. Note that all components, except the two side components at each end, require four side beads.

2) Working off a corner bead in either direction, add the next component. Continue to add components in a zigzagging fashion until your center row has 14 components and the edge rows each have 13 components.

3) Add the partial components on the edges:

• Exiting a corner A on an edge component, work a RAW stitch with two Bs and an A, and then work the second RAW stitch with three Bs **(figure 21)**.

• Add a B, an A, a B, and an A between the existing beads, exiting the first new B **(figure 22)**.

• Make a connecting RAW stitch attaching it to the corresponding corner bead in the next component with a B and an A. Sew through to exit the new A **(figure 23, a–b)**. Pick up a C, and sew through the next A and B **(b–c)**. Continue through the beadwork to exit the corresponding corner A on the next edge component.

4) Repeat step 3 along the other edge.

5) Make a clasp component, attach it with a single connection, and make a single connection loop.

11° seed beads
○ color A
◑ color B
○ color C

Peyote with a twist (Peytwist)

techniques by
Gerlinde Lenz

materials

beginner zigzag bracelet
8¼ in. (21 cm)

- 11º seed beads
  - **3 g** color A (Toho PF552, permanent finish galvanized sweet blush)
  - **7 g** color B (Toho 2634F, semi-glazed turquoise AB)
  - **3 g** color C (Miyuki 596, opaque tea rose luster)
- **2** 6 mm jump rings
- **1** toggle clasp
- Fireline, 6 lb. test
- beading needles, #11 or #12
- **2** pairs of chainnose, bent-nose, and/or flatnose pliers

wrapped in flowers necklace (p. 25)

red/green/blue colors
21 in. (53 cm)

- 11º seed beads
  - **4 g** color A (Toho 29AF, silver-lined frosted black diamond)
  - **5 g** color B (Toho 25CF, silver-lined frosted ruby)
  - **1 g** color C (Miyuki 4F, matte silver-lined dark gold)
  - **10 g** color D (Toho 24BF, silver-lined tr. matte peridot)
  - **5 g** color E (Toho 33F, silver-lined matte light cobalt)
  - **5 g** color F (Toho 35F, silver-lined matte sapphire)

Find info for the alternate colorway at

FacetJewelry.com/resourceguide

basics

- peyote stitch: flat even-count
- attaching a stop bead
- ending and adding thread

This new technique, "peyote with a twist — not crochet" (Peytwist for the remainder of this article) was developed by Gerlinde Lenz which uses peyote stitch to achieve the same look as bead-single crochet. It is easy to learn and works up quickly. There are two different techniques of Peytwist: the single-column seam, which is shared here (with Gerlinde's blessing, of course!), and the double-column seam (p. 26). Peytwist starts with a flat even-count swatch of peyote-stitched beadwork. The width and number of rows can vary between designs. To learn the technique, you will start with a piece that is 10 beads wide and seven rows long.

BEGINNER ZIGZAG BRACELET

Starter strip

1) On a comfortable length of thread, attach a stop bead, leaving a 12-in. (30 cm) tail. Starting at the upper-right corner of **figure 1**, pick up a color A 11º seed bead, eight color B 11º seed beads, and an A.
2) Following the **pattern** or the Word chart (available at FacetJewelry.com/resourceguide), work five rows in flat even-count peyote stitch to create a swatch with a total of seven rows **(figure 1)**. Remove the stop bead.

Joining the strip

Position your beadwork with the tail in the upper right-hand corner and your working thread in the lower right-hand corner. With the working thread and leaving the beadwork flat, cross over the beadwork diagonally, and sew through the A in the upper left-hand corner, with your needle pointing away from the bead-work **(figure 2, a–b)**. Cross back over the beadwork, and sew through the last bead added (last up-bead) in the seventh row, with the needle pointing toward the center of the beadwork **(b–c)**. Tighten the bead-work to curve the corners upward and bring them together **(photo a)**. Turn the beadwork so the tail is now positioned downward and the working thread is still exiting the B **(figure 3 and photo b)**.

a

b

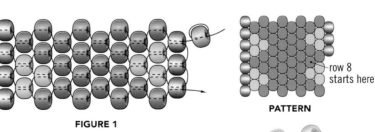

row 8 starts here

FIGURE 1

PATTERN

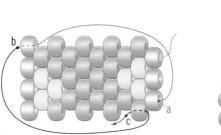

FIGURE 2

FIGURE 3

	11º seed bead, color A
	11º seed bead, color B
	11º seed bead, color C

Adding rows

You will now begin working rows of peyote stitch along the top edge of the tube. Do not use tight tension when stitching the rope; an even, moderate tension works best. When adding rows that go left, the beads will be added as you move up toward the point of the beadwork. When adding rows that go right, the beads will be added as you move down toward the V in the beadwork. As you finish the row heading downward, you will be attaching it to the seam beads. The color A beads in this pattern will be your seam beads.

1) Work row 8 in peyote stitch to the left (or upward): Pick up a B, and sew through the next B (**figure 3 and photo c**). Repeat this stitch three more times, sewing through the A at the tip for the last stitch (**figure 4 and photo d**).

2) Work row 9 in peyote stitch to the right (or downward): one A, and three Bs (**figure 5**).

3) To work the last stitch in row 9 and work a turn, pick up a C. If you look at the beads near the V in the beadwork in **figure 6**, you will notice that the last down-bead (outlined in green) is sitting adja-

FIGURE 4

FIGURE 5

FIGURE 6

cent to two seam beads (outlined in red). Sew down through the upper of these two seam beads (**a–b and photo e**). Continue up through the following A seam bead above the one your thread is exiting (outlined in blue), and sew back through the C just added to step up and be in position to start the next row (**b–c and photo f**).

4) You are now ready to start row 10 (**photo g**). Work as in steps 1–3, following the pattern or word chart for rows 10–13, and then repeat rows 8–13 for the desired length of the rope, allowing approximately 1¼ in. (3.2 cm) for the clasp. End and add thread as needed.

tip When ending and adding thread, do not end the original working thread until you have added a new working thread and it is exiting the same bead your

original working thread is exiting. Then end the original working thread.

Ending the rope

You need to fill in the V area at the end of the rope to close it off evenly without adding more length before attaching a clasp.

1) Follow the established color pattern with these changes:
• Work an upward (left) row of peyote with three stitches instead of four (**photo h**).
• Work a downward row with four stitches instead of five.
• Work an upward row with two stitches.
• Work a downward row with three stitches.
• Work an upward row with one stitch.
• Work a downward row with two stitches.

2) Sew through the up-beads at the end of the rope to draw them into a ring, and retrace the thread path to tighten.

3) Pick up five As, and sew through the opposite bead in the ring to form a loop. Continue back through the beads just added and the bead your thread exited at the start of this step, going in the same direction (**photo i**). Retrace the thread path through the loop, and end the working thread.

4) With the tail thread exiting the tip bead, work as before to add one more downward row following the established pattern. Repeat steps 1–3 to complete this end of the rope. End the tail.

5) Open a jump ring, and attach half of the clasp to the loop on one end of the rope. Repeat at the other end of the rope.

c

d

e

f

g

Tips for single-column seam patterns

• If you lose your place while stitching a pattern, look at the last couple of rows you stitched on the inside of the tube, not the outside of the tube. The inside of the tube reflects the pattern as it is stitched. The outside is a mirror image of the pattern.

• The number of beads per row and the number of rows needed before joining may vary between patterns, which will change the diameter of the rope. Other beads like 15º and 8º seed beads and cylinder beads can be used in Peytwist patterns.

h

i

wrapped in flowers necklace

Now that you've mastered the basic technique, try this flowered pattern by Gerlinde Lenz. It will start the same as the beginner zigzag pattern with a piece of peyote that is 10 beads wide and seven rows long. Join the beadwork as before after row 7. Continue the pattern starting with row 8. The seam beads will have a variety of colors, not just one like on the beginner pattern, so follow the pattern or word chart carefully. The Word chart is available at FacetJewelry.com/resourceguide. End the necklace the same way as the beginner pattern.

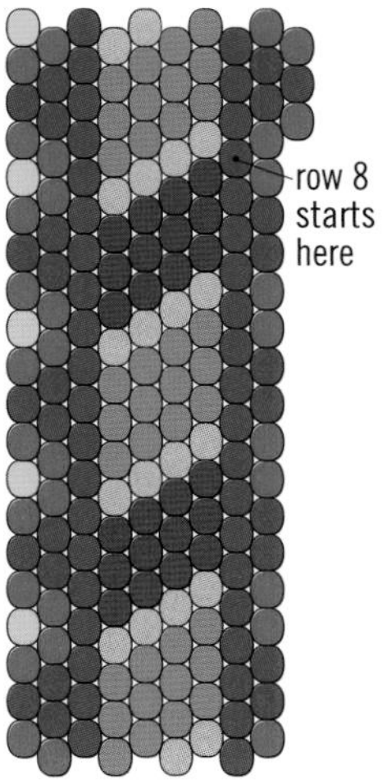

row 8 starts here

PATTERN

11º seed beads
- color A
- color B
- color C
- color D
- color E
- color F

Double-column seam Peytwist

techniques by Gerlinde Lenz

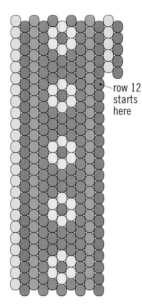

→row 12 starts here

PATTERN

materials

green/brown necklace 21 in. (53 cm)

- 11º seed beads
  - **5 g** color A (Miyuki 1F, matte silver-lined crystal)
  - **9 g** color B (Miyuki 5F, matte silver-lined dark topaz)
  - **2 g** color C (Toho 30BF, matte silver-lined hyacinth)
  - **9 g** color D (Toho 989F, frosted gold-lined crystal)
  - **5 g** color E (Toho 999F, matte bronze-lined black diamond)
  - **10 g** color F (Toho 37F, matte silver-lined olivine)
- **2** 6 mm jump rings
- **1** toggle clasp
- Fireline, 6 lb. test
- beading needles, #11 or #12
- **2** pairs of chainnose, bent nose, and/or flatnose pliers

Find info for the alternate colorway at
FacetJewelry.com/
resourceguide

basics

- peyote stitch: flat even-count
- attaching a stop bead
- ending and adding thread

○ 11º seed bead, color A

● 11º seed bead, color B

● 11º seed bead, color C

● 11º seed bead, color D

○ 11º seed bead, color E

● 11º seed bead, color F

There are two different techniques for Peytwist. The reason there are two different techniques is because some patterns have an even number of beads in the circumference and some have an odd number, just like there is an even and odd flat peyote stitch. Single-column Peytwist is used for an odd number of beads in the circumference, and double-column is used for an even number. Start with a flat even-count strip of peyote-stitched beadwork. The width and the number of rows can vary between

designs. This pattern by Gerlinde Lenz starts with a strip that is 12 beads wide and 11 rows long.

COUNTRY STYLE NECKLACE
Starter strip

1) On a comfortable length of thread, attach a stop bead, leaving a 12-in. (30 cm) tail. Starting at the upper-right corner of **figure 1**, pick up a color B 11º seed bead, a color E 11º seed bead, a B, a color D 11º seed bead, two color F 11º seed beads, a color A 11º seed bead, two Fs, a D, a B, and an E.

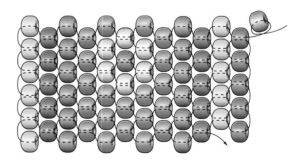

FIGURE 1

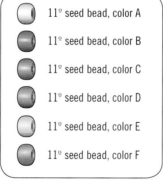

b

a   c

FIGURE 2

a

2) Following the **pattern** or the Word Chart (available at FacetJewelry.com/resourceguide), work nine rows in flat even-count peyote stitch to create a strip with a total of 11 rows, adding only five beads instead of six in row 11 **(figure 1)**.

Joining the strip
1) Position your beadwork with the tail in the upper right-hand corner and your working thread on the lower right of the strip.
2) With the working thread and leaving the beadwork flat, cross

over the beadwork diagonally, and sew through the E in the upper left-hand corner, with your needle pointing toward the opposite edge **(figure 2, a–b)**. Cross back over the beadwork, and sew through last up-bead in row 10, with your needle pointing away from the beadwork **(b–c)**. The top-left E will fit into the remaining open space of row 11 to complete that row. Tighten the beadwork to curve the corners upward and bring them together **(photo a)**. Turn the beadwork so the tail is now positioned downward and the working thread is still exiting the B **(figure 3,** outlined in red, and **photo b)**. The columns of Es and Bs at the join are your seam beads.
3) Sew up through the adjacent B **(figure 4,** outlined in blue and shown slightly out of position for

thread path clarity) and the E **(figure 4,** outlined in green) that fit into the open space of row 11 **(photo c)**. This will be your starting point to begin row 12.

Adding rows
You will now begin working rows of peyote stitch along the top edge of the tube. When adding rows that go left, the beads will be added as you move up toward the point of the beadwork. When adding rows that go right, the beads will be added as you move down toward the V in the beadwork. As you finish the row heading downward, you will be attaching it to the seam beads.
1) Work row 12 in peyote stitch to the left (or upward) as follows:
• Pick up a B, and sew through the next D.

• Pick up an F, and sew through the next F.
• Pick up an A, and sew through the next F.
• Pick up a F, and sew through the next D.
• Pick up a B, and sew through the next E **(figure 5** and **photo d)**.
2) Work row 13 in peyote stitch to the right (or downward) as follows: an E, a D, two As, and a D **(figure 6** and **photo e)**.
3) To work the double-column seam turn: If you look at the beads near the V in the beadwork, you will notice the B your thread is exiting is near two Es. Sew through the E that is slightly above your B **(figure 7,** outlined in red). This E is sitting adjacent to two B seam beads **(figure 7,** outlined in blue). Sew down through the lower B and up through the upper B. Continue back up through the adjacent E you

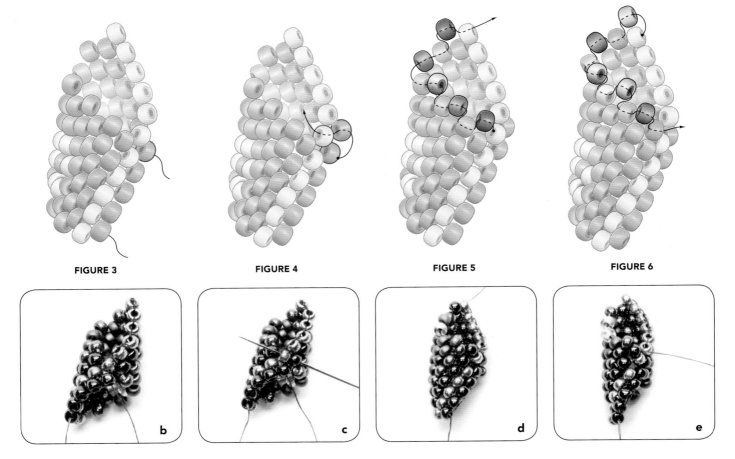

FIGURE 3   **FIGURE 4**   **FIGURE 5**   **FIGURE 6**

b   c   d   e

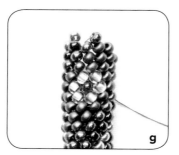

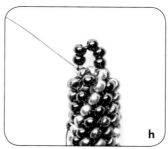

FIGURE 7

just sewed through **(figure 7** and **photo f)**. This gets you in position to start the next row.

4) Continue working in peyote stitch following the pattern or Word Chart for the desired length of the rope, allowing approximately 1¼ in. (3.2 cm) for the clasp. End and add thread as needed.

tip When ending and adding thread, do not end the original working thread until you have added a new working thread and it is exiting the same bead your original working thread is exiting. Then end the original working thread.

Ending the rope

You need to fill in the V area at the end of the rope to close it off evenly without adding more length before attaching a clasp.

1) Follow the established color

pattern with these changes:
• Work an upward (left) row of peyote with four stitches instead of five.
• Work a downward row with four stitches instead of five **(photo g)**.
• Work an upward row with three stitches.
• Work a downward row with three stitches.
• Work an upward row with two stitches.
• Work a downward row with two stitches.
• Work an upward row with one stitch.
• Work a downward row with one stitch.

2) Sew through the beadwork to exit an end up-bead. Continue through the up-beads at the end of the rope to draw them into a ring, and retrace the thread path to tighten.

3) Pick up five As, and sew through the two opposite beads in the ring to form a loop. Continue back through the beads just added and the bead your thread exited at the start of this step, going in the same direction **(photo h)**. Retrace the thread path through the loop, and end the working thread.

4) Remove the stop bead from the tail. Work as before to add one more downward row following the established pattern. Repeat steps 1–3 to complete this end of the rope. End the tail.

5) Open a jump ring, and attach half of the clasp to the loop on one end of the rope. Repeat at the other end of the rope.

Word chart»

If you prefer to use a Word Chart instead of the pattern, find it at FacetJewelry.com/resourcesguide.

Projects

Funky hearts
bracelet
by Lorraine Coetzee

materials
bracelet 7½ in. (19.1 cm)

- 11º Miyuki Delica cylinder beads
  - **2 g** color A (DB0200, opaque chalk white)
  - **3 g** color B (DB0042, gold-lined crystal)
  - **4 g** color C (DB0859, matte emerald AB)
  - **3 g** color D (DB0074, lined light fuchsia AB)
  - **3 g** color E (DB0795, matte opaque vermillion)
  - **2 g** color F (DB0654, dark cranberry opaque)
- Fireline, 6 lb. test, or nylon beading thread, size D
- beading needles, #12

basics
- peyote stitch: flat, even-count, flat odd-count, zipping up or joining
- ending and adding thread
- attaching a stop bead

For a Word chart of this pattern, visit **FacetJewelry. com/resourceguide**

PATTERN

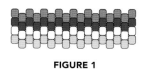

FIGURE 1

FIGURE 2   **FIGURE 3**

Show your wild side with this heart-motif bracelet that is bursting with vibrant colors.

PEYOTE BAND

1) On a comfortable length of thread, attach a stop bead, leaving a 6-in. (15 cm) tail. Starting at the upper-right corner of the pattern, pick up 11º cylinder beads for rows 1 and 2: one B, eight As, one B, 10 Cs, one B, and seven As.

2) Following the **pattern** or the Word chart (get it at FacetJewelry.com/resourceguide), work in flat even-count peyote stitch using the appropriate color cylinders. End and add thread as needed while you stitch, and end the working thread and tail when you complete the band.

EDGING

1) Add a comfortable length of thread to one end of the band, and exit the nearest corner cylinder, with your needle pointing away from the beadwork.

2) Pick up three cylinders in colors that match the adjacent cylinders in the band, and sew down through the next edge cylinder and up through the following edge cylinder. Repeat this stitch for the length of the band, picking up colors to extend the design into the edging.

3) Sew through the beadwork to exit the nearest corner cylinder along the other edge, and repeat step 2. End and add thread as needed.

CLASP

1) Refer to **figure 1**: On 18 in. (46 cm) of thread, attach a stop bead, leaving a 6-in. (15 cm) tail. Pick up 17 color D cylinders. Using Cs, work two rows of flat odd-count peyote stitch. Repeat to work two rows with As and two rows with Bs. Zip up the edges to form the toggle bar, and end the working thread and tail.

2) Add 12 in. (30 cm) of thread to one end of the band, and exit one of the middle up-beads in the end row. Pick up six cylinders to match the cylinder you thread is exiting, and sew through a middle cylinder on the toggle bar. Sew back through the sixth cylinder, and then work three peyote stitches, sewing into the adjacent middle up-bead in the end row of the band **(figure 2)**.

3) Add 12 in. (30 cm) of thread to the other end of the band, and exit one up-bead away from the middle up-bead. Pick up approximately 23 Cs, skip the middle up-bead, and sew through the following up-bead to form a loop **(figure 3, a–b)**. Work back around the loop in peyote stitch, using one C per stitch, and sew through the bead your thread exited at the start of this step **(b–c)**. Retrace the thread path through the loop a couple of times, and end the thread.

Carrier bead beauties necklace

Unpretentious and pillow-shaped, carrier beads have taken bead shops, groups, and societies by storm. Explore this fun new way to make quick and easy beaded beads in unlimited patterns.

by Julia Gerlach and Diane Jolie

So what are carrier beads, you ask?

Also known as carrier duo base beads, carrier pillow beads, and Trägerperlen, they are glass — produced in the Czech Republic — or acrylic — produced in China — beads that are used to support zipped peyote strips (or other stitched strips) to form beaded beads. They measure 17 x 9 x 5 mm, are tapered on each end, and have two holes that accommodate stringing material up to 2 mm thick. Available in a wide array of colors, they are now appearing in your favorite beads stores and online bead merchants.

MAKE A BEADED BEAD

Making a beaded bead with a carrier bead is as simple as creating a small peyote strip, and zipping it up around the carrier bead. The most common bead to use for this strip is the 11º cylinder bead, though you can certainly try other beads, as will be discussed in a bit.

1) On 1 yd. (.9 m) of thread, pick up six 11º cylinder beads (**figure 1, a–b**). Use a single color or follow a pattern (see **patterns**, top left). These beads will form the first two rows as the next row in added.

2) Pick up a cylinder, skip the last cylinder in the group of six, and sew back through the next cylinder (**b–c**). Pick up a cylinder, skip the next cylinder, and sew through the following one. Repeat this stitch once more (**c–d**). This completes row 3.

3) To begin the next row, pick up a cylinder, and sew through the last bead added in the previous row (**d–e**). Continue working across the row in flat even-count peyote (**e–f**) until you have 48 or 50 rows (24 or 25 beads on each long edge), working three stitches per row. Wrap the strip around a carrier bead to make sure it fits, and add or remove two rows if necessary. If desired, place a bit of jewelry glue or double-sided tape (like Thermo-O-Web, Wonder Tape, or redline tape) on the carrier bead, and then zip up the ends of the peyote strip to form a continuous band around the carrier bead. End the threads.

materials
flat peyote carrier bead with 11º cylinders

- **1** carrier bead
- **1 g** 11º cylinder beads (Miyuki Delicas) in colors of your choice
- Fireline, 6 lb. test
- beading needles, #12
- jewelry glue or double-sided tape (optional)

basics

- peyote stitch: flat even-count, flat odd-count, zipping up or joining
- ending and adding thread

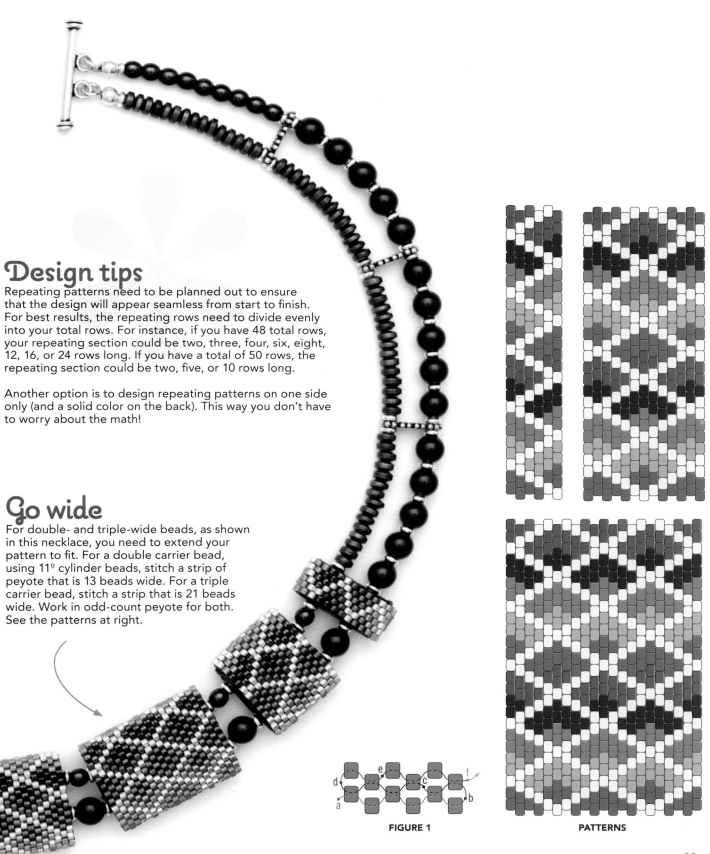

Design tips

Repeating patterns need to be planned out to ensure that the design will appear seamless from start to finish. For best results, the repeating rows need to divide evenly into your total rows. For instance, if you have 48 total rows, your repeating section could be two, three, four, six, eight, 12, 16, or 24 rows long. If you have a total of 50 rows, the repeating section could be two, five, or 10 rows long.

Another option is to design repeating patterns on one side only (and a solid color on the back). This way you don't have to worry about the math!

Go wide

For double- and triple-wide beads, as shown in this necklace, you need to extend your pattern to fit. For a double carrier bead, using 11º cylinder beads, stitch a strip of peyote that is 13 beads wide. For a triple carrier bead, stitch a strip that is 21 beads wide. Work in odd-count peyote for both. See the patterns at right.

FIGURE 1

PATTERNS

FINDING OR CREATING PATTERNS

Carrier bead patterns are widely available. Go to Pinterest, Etsy, or your local bead shop to find patterns in all varies — stripes, dots, flowers, and much more! If you'd rather graph your own patterns, you have a few options.

- Use a graphing software like Bead Tool or Easy Bead Patterns to create your own look.
- Download blank graph paper at FacetJewelry.com/resources, and then use colored pencils to design to your heart's content.

A few design options

- Use 10–15 carrier beads to make a bracelet
- Use 25–35 carrier beads to make a necklace
- Use 9–13 carrier beads to form just the focal point of a necklace
- Make double- or triple-wide beaded beads by making a wider strip of beadwork. Use double-sided tape to join two or three carrier beads side-by-side, and then wrap the extended bead in the peyote strip.
- Try something completely different! Use two-hole beads, Demi beads, quarter Tilas, or fire-polished beads, as shown in these examples.

BEAD TYPE	BEADS ACROSS	ROWS	SAMPLE
11º cylinder beads	6	48 or 50	
11º seed beads	6	42	
15º seed beads	8	52 or 54	
15º cylinder beads	8	64	
10º cylinder beads	5*	42	
3 mm bugle beads	3*	50	

*Work in odd-count flat peyote

Mediterranean triangle
earrings

by June Malone

The intricate pattern stands out with these three-dimensional colorful earrings.

1

BASE

1) Work in rounds, stepping up through the first cylinder added in each round, and ending and adding thread as needed.

Round 1: On 4 ft. (1.2 m) of thread, pick up three color A 11º cylinder beads, and tie them into a ring with a square knot, leaving a 6-in. (15 cm) tail. Sew through the first A again.

Round 2: Pick up two color B 11º cylinder beads, and sew through the next A to form a herringbone corner stitch **(figure 1, a–b)**. Repeat this stitch twice to complete the round **(b–c)**. Throughout the project, the corner stitches will be made with two Bs per stitch.

Round 3: Work a corner stitch **(c–d)** and a peyote stitch using a color C 11º cylinder bead **(d–e)**. Repeat these stitches twice to complete the round **(e–f)**.

Round 4: Work a corner stitch and two peyote stitches using a C for each stitch **(f–g)**. Repeat these stitches twice to complete the round **(g–h)**.

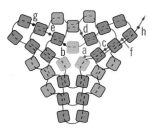

FIGURE 1

2) For the remaining rounds, first work a corner stitch (CS), and then work peyote stitches with the following beads using one bead per stitch. Repeat the stitches twice to complete the round, and step up:

Round 5: CS, one C, one color D 11º cylinder bead, and one C **(figure 2, a–b)**.

Round 6: CS, one C, two Ds, and one C **(b–c)**.

Round 7: CS, one C, one D, one color E 11º cylinder bead, one D, and one C **(c–d)**.

Round 8: CS, one E, one D, two Es, one D, and one E **(d–e)**.

Round 9: CS, one E, one D, one E, one A, one E, one D, and one E **(e–f)**.

Round 10: CS, three Es, two color F 11º cylinder beads, and three Es **(f–g)**.

Round 11: CS, two Fs, one E, one F, one A, one F, one E, two Fs **(g–h)**.

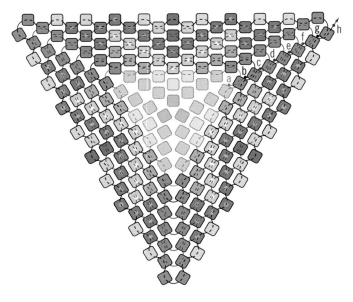

FIGURE 2

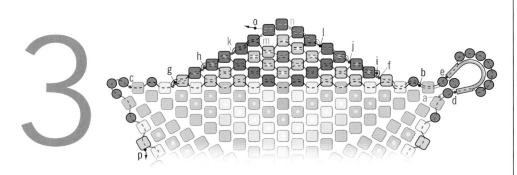

FIGURE 3

FIGURE 4

3) Pick up three 15º seed beads, and sew through the adjacent B **(figure 3, a–b)**. Work nine peyote stitches with the following beads: one 15º, three Fs, two As, three Fs, and one 15º **(b–c)**. Repeat these stitches twice to complete the round, and step up through the first 15º added **(c–d)**.

4) Pick up one end of a wire guard and seven 15ºs, and sew through the other end of the wire guard **(d–e)**. Continue through the next five beads as shown **(e–f)**.

5) Work seven peyote stitches using one E, one F, one A, one D, one A, one F, and one E **(f–g)**. Make a decrease turn to reverse direction: Sew around the closest thread bridge, sew back through the bead your thread is exiting, and step up through the last bead added **(g–h)**.

6) Work six peyote stitches using one E, one A, two Ds, one A, and one E **(h–i)**. Work a decrease turn to reverse direction **(i–j)**.

7) Work five peyote stitches using one E, one D, one B, one D, and one E. Work a decrease turn to reverse direction **(j–k)**.

8) Work four peyote stitches using one A, two Ds, and one A. Work a decrease turn to reverse direction **(k–l)**.

9) Work three peyote stitches using one A, one D, and one A. Work a decrease stitch to reverse direction **(l–m)**.

10) Work two peyote stitches with one A each. Work a decrease turn to reverse direction **(m–n)**.

11) Work a peyote stitch using one A **(n–o)**.

12) Sew through the beadwork as needed to exit the next F "up" bead on the following edge **(point p)**, and work as in steps 5–11 to complete this edge. Repeat this step once to complete the remaining edge, and end the threads.

EMBELLISHMENT AND FLAPS

1) Attach 1 yd. (.9 m) of thread to the beadwork, exiting an A in the center ring of As **(figure 4, point a)**.

2) Pick up a 5 mm bead cap, a 4 mm round faceted crystal, and a 15º, and sew back through the crystal and the bead cap **(a–b)** to form a center accent. Continue through the same A your thread exited at the start of this step, going in the same direction, and the following A in the center ring **(b–c)**. Attach the center accent as before to the remaining center As.

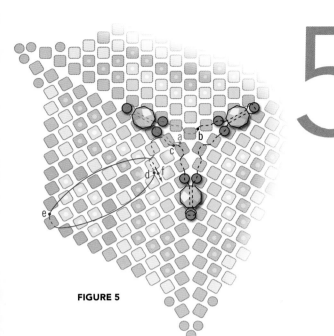

FIGURE 5

5

3) Sew up through the adjacent B in the closest herringbone stitch, pick up a 15º, a 3 mm fire-polished bead, and a 15º, and sew back through the 3 mm. Pick up a 15º, and sew down through the adjacent B in the same herringbone stitch and the next A in the center ring to form a small fringe **(figure 5, a–b)**. The center accent isn't shown in the figure for clarity. Pull the thread tight. Repeat this stitch twice to complete the round **(b–c)**.

4) To secure the flaps: Sew through the beadwork as shown, exiting the D closest to the center **(c–d)**. Gently fold the corresponding edge over, and align the tip A bead with the same D. Sew through the tip A **(d–e)**, continue through the D your thread was exiting, going in the same direction **(e–f)**, and pull the thread tight. Retrace the thread path to secure the connection, and sew through the beadwork as needed to exit the corresponding D on the next edge. Work as before to secure the remaining two flaps.

5) Open the loop of an ear wire, and attach it to the wire guard loop.

6) Make another earring.

	4 mm round faceted crystal
	3 mm fire-polished bead

11º cylinder beads

	color A
	color B
	color C
	color D
	color E
	color F
	15º seed bead

materials
earrings 1⁵⁄₁₆ x 1¼ in. (3.3 x 3.2 cm)

- **2** 4 mm round faceted crystals (Swarovski, lilac shadow)
- **6** 3 mm fire-polished beads (Czech, green turquoise Picasso)
- 11º cylinder beads (Miyuki Delica)
  - **1 g** color A (DB0022, metallic dark bronze)
  - **1 g** color B (DB1991, metallic French plum)
  - **1 g** color C (DB0264, opaque mallard luster)
  - **1 g** color D (DB0263, opaque cactus luster)
  - **1 g** color E (DB0788, dyed semi-frosted transparent dark teal)
  - **1 g** color F (DB1832F, Duracoat galvanized matte gold)
- **1 g** 15º seed beads (Miyuki 457, metallic dark bronze)
- **2** 5 mm bead caps
- **1** pair of earring findings
- **2** wire guards
- Fireline, 6 lb. test
- beading needles, #11 or #12
- **2** pairs of chainnose, flatnose, and/or bentnose pliers

Kits are available at enchantedbeadsbyjm.etsy.com

basics
- peyote stitch: flat
- herringbone stitch
- ending and adding thread
- square knot

Endless diamond
bangles   by Regina Payne

Peyote diamonds form a base that supports a continuous pattern of crystal and pearl clusters.

BASE

1) On a comfortable length of thread, pick up a repeating pattern of five color A 11º cylinder beads and a color B 11º cylinder bead 26 times for a 3-in. (7.6 cm) diameter bangle.

tip Test the fit to see if the strand will fit around the widest part of your hand. Adjust the number of repeats by an even number to adjust the size.

Center the beads on the thread, and wrap the tail on a thread bobbin or piece of cardboard. These beads will shift to form rows 1 and 2 as the next row is added. End and add thread throughout the beadwork as needed.

2) Work row 3 in flat even-count peyote stitch, following a repeating pattern of one stitch using a B and two stitches using As **(figure 1, a–b)**. Keep your tension even, and make sure the beadwork is not twisted.

3) Join the ends together by sewing through the first B added in row 3 on the opposite end as shown **(b–c)**, making sure the beadwork is not twisted. Unwind the tail, and attach a needle. With the tail thread, repeat the join, but sew through the B adjacent to the one your working thread is exiting.

4) With each needle, work in tubular peyote stitch as follows, and step up at the end of each round:

Rounds 4 and 5: Work three stitches using a B, an A, and a B. Repeat these stitches to complete the round **(figure 2, a–b and aa–bb)**.

Rounds 6 and 7: Work two stitches using one B per stitch and one using a color C 11º cylinder bead. Repeat these stitches to complete the round **(b–c and bb–cc)**.

Rounds 8 and 9: Work one stitch using a B and two using Cs. Repeat these stitches to complete the round **(c–d and cc–dd)**.

materials
purple bangle 3-in. (7.6 cm) diameter

- **52** 4 mm crystal pearls (Swarovski, cream)
- **52** 4 mm crystal bicones (Swarovski, tanzanite)
- **13** 3 mm crystal bicones (Swarovski, purple velvet)
- **26** 2 mm glass pearls (white)
- 11º cylinder beads
  - **2 g** color A (Miyuki Delica DB0284, sparkle purple-lined aqua luster)
  - **3 g** color B (Miyuki Delica DB0042, silver-lined gold)
  - **2 g** color C (Miyuki Delica DB0221, gilt-lined white opal)
- **2 g** 15º seed beads (Toho PF557, galvanized starlight)
- Fireline, 8 or 6 lb. test
- beading needles, #11 or #12
- thread bobbin or piece of cardboard

Find info for the alternate colorways at FacetJewelry.com/resourceguide

basics
- peyote stitch: flat even-count, forming a strip into a ring, tubular
- ending and adding thread

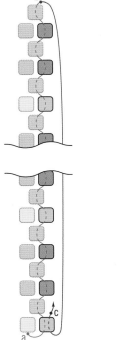

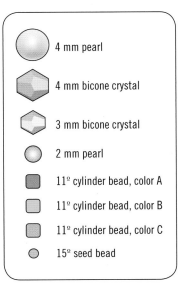

⬤	4 mm pearl
⬣	4 mm bicone crystal
⬣	3 mm bicone crystal
●	2 mm pearl
▪	11º cylinder bead, color A
▫	11º cylinder bead, color B
▫	11º cylinder bead, color C
○	15º seed bead

FIGURE 1

FIGURE 2

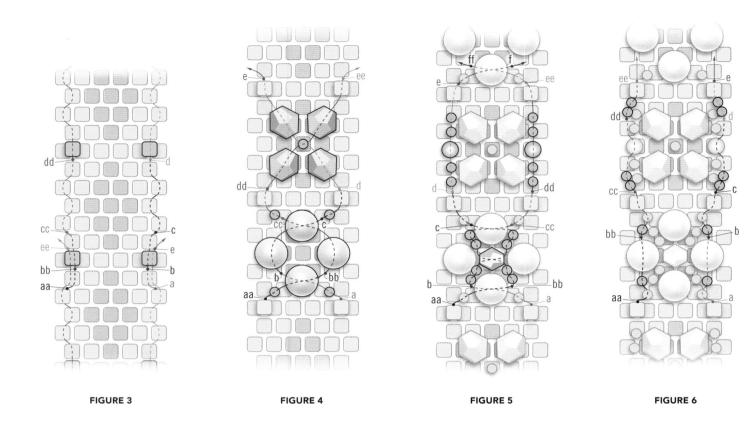

FIGURE 3   **FIGURE 4**   **FIGURE 5**   **FIGURE 6**

Rounds 10 and 11: Work three stitches using a B, a C, and a B. Repeat these stitches to complete the round **(d–e and dd–ee)**, and sew through the next C **(figure 3, a–b and aa–bb)**.

5) With each needle, pick up a B, skip the next C, and sew through the following C so the B sits on top of the base **(b–c and bb–cc)**. Continue through the next four beads **(c–d and cc–dd)**. Repeat these stitches to complete the round, and sew through the first raised B added in this round **(d–e and dd–ee)**.

EMBELLISHMENT

1) With one needle, pick up a 15º seed bead and a 4 mm pearl **(figure 4, a–b)**. With the other needle, pick up a 15º, and cross through the 4 mm pearl just added **(aa–bb)**. With one needle, pick up two 4 mm pearls **(b–c)**. With the other needle, pick up a 4 mm pearl, and cross through the last 4 mm pearl added **(bb–cc)**. With each needle, pick up a 15º, and sew through the next raised B added on the base **(c–d and cc–dd)**.

2) With one needle, pick up a 4 mm bicone crystal, a 15º, and a 4 mm crystal, cross to the other side of the base, and sew through the next raised B **(d–e)**. With the other needle, pick up 4 mm crystal, sew through the center 15º added in the previous stitch, pick up a 4 mm crystal, and sew through the following raised B on the opposite side of the base **(dd–ee)**.

3) Repeat steps 1–2 for the remainder of the base. With each thread, sew through the next 15º, and cross through the first 4 mm pearl **(figure 5, a–b and aa–bb)**.

4) With one needle, pick up two 15ºs, a 3 mm bicone crystal, and two 15ºs, cross the pearl embellishment diagonally, and sew through the opposite 4 mm pearl, going in the same direction **(b–c)**. With the other needle, pick up two 15ºs, sew through the 3 mm crystal, pick up two 15ºs, and cross through the opposite 4 mm pearl, going in the same direction **(bb–cc)**. With each needle, sew through the next 15º and raised B **(c–d and cc–dd)**.

5) With each needle, pick up two 15ºs, a 2 mm pearl, and two 15ºs, skip the next two 4 mm crystals, and sew through the following raised B **(d–e and dd–ee)**. With each needle, sew through the next 15º, and cross through the 4 mm pearl **(e–f and ee–ff)**.

6) Repeat steps 4–5 for the remainder of the base, but after the last stitch, do not sew through the next 15º and pearl.

7) With each needle, sew through the adjacent 15º, pick up a 15º, and sew through the next edge 4 mm pearl **(figure 6, a–b and aa–bb)**. Pick up a 15º, and sew through the following 15º and raised B **(b–c and bb–cc)**.

8) With each needle, pick up two 15ºs, skip the next C in the base, and sew through the following B on the outside edge of the base, the 2 mm pearl in the embellishment, and the next B on the outside edge of the base **(c–d and cc–dd)**. Pick up two 15ºs, and sew through the following raised B **(d–e and dd–ee)**.

9) Repeat steps 7–8 for the remainder of the base using an even tension, and end the threads.

Go fish
bracelet
by Kristy Zgoda

materials
bracelet 7 in. (18 cm)

- **8** 4 mm fire-polished beads (lime opal)
- **11⁰** Miyuki Delica cylinder beads
  - **1 g** color A (DB0733, opaque chartreuse)
  - **1 g** color B (DB0010, opaque black)
  - **2 g** color C (DB1345, silver-lined bright violet)
  - **5 g** color D (DB0310, matte black)
  - **1 g** color E (DB0724, opaque pea green)
  - **1 g** color F (DB1379, opaque red-violet)
  - **1 g** color G (DB1840F, galvanized baby pink)
  - **1 g** color H (DB0651, opaque squash)
  - **1 g** color I (DB0727, opaque light Siam)
  - **1 g** color J (DB0164, opaque light blue AB)
  - **1 g** color K (DB0760, matte opaque light sapphire)
  - **1 g** color L (DB0721, opaque yellow)
  - **1 g** color M (DB0681, semi-matte silver-lined squash)
  - **1 g** color N (DB0150, silver-lined bronze)
  - **1 g** color O (DB1340, silver-lined bright fuchsia)
  - **1 g** color P (DB1511, matte opaque pale yellow)
  - **1 g** color Q (DB1523, matte opaque light salmon AB)
  - **1 g** color R (DB1517, matte opaque light sky blue)
  - **1 g** color S (DB1363, opaque peach)
  - **1 g** color T (DB0200, opaque chalk white)
- **1** four-strand slide clasp (purple, metaldesinz.com)
- beading needles, #10
- Fireline, 6 lb. test, or nylon beading thread, size D

Get a Word chart for this pattern at **FacetJewelry.com/resourceguide**

basics
- peyote stitch: flat, even-count
- attaching a stop bead
- ending and adding thread

Stitch up this bracelet featuring a lively school of fish in a bright array of colors.

PEYOTE BAND

1) On a comfortable length of thread, attach a stop bead, leaving a 6-in. (15 cm) tail. Starting at the upper-right corner of the pattern, pick up 11⁰ cylinder beads for rows 1 and 2: one A, one C, 18 Ds, one C, and one A.

2) Following the **pattern** or the Word chart (get it at FacetJewelry.com/resourceguide), work in flat even-count peyote stitch using the appropriate color cylinders. End and add thread as needed while you stitch, and end the working thread and tail when you complete the band.

CLASP

Add a new 1-ft. (30 cm) thread to one end of the beadwork, and exit the third up-bead from the edge that ends with an up-bead **(figure 1, point a)**. Pick up a 4 mm fire-polished bead and the end loop of a slide clasp. Sew back through the 4 mm, and continue through the next three end beads in the band **(a–b)**. Repeat this stitch three times to attach each clasp loop to the band **(b–c)**. Retrace the thread path through the clasp connections at least once, and end the thread. Repeat at the other end to attach the other clasp half.

11⁰ cylinder beads
- ▣ color A
- ▣ color B
- ▣ color C
- ◼ color D
- ▣ color E
- ▣ color F
- ▣ color G
- ▣ color H
- ▣ color I
- ▣ color J
- ▣ color K
- ▣ color L
- ▣ color M
- ▣ color N
- ▣ color O
- ▢ color P
- ▣ color Q
- ▢ color R
- ▣ color S
- ▢ color T

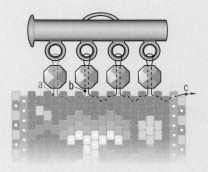

FIGURE 1

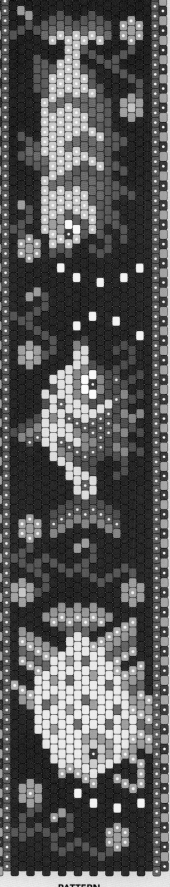

PATTERN

Stacked diamonds
bracelet by June Malone

materials
bracelet 6¾ in (17.1 cm)

- 5 x 1.2 mm Quarter-Tila beads
  - **1 g** color C, nickel plated
  - **1 g** color E, turquoise
- 11º cylinder beads (Miyuki Delica)
  - **2 g** color A (DB1158, galvanized semi-frosted light smoky amethyst)
  - **6 g** color B (DB1852, Duracoat galvanized pewter)
  - **1 g** color D (DB0878, matte opaque turquoise green AB)
  - **1 g** color F (DB1165, galvanized matte muscat)
  - **1 g** color G (DB1843, Duracoat galvanized dark mauve)
  - **1 g** color H (DB0310, matte black)
- **2 g** 15º seed beads, color I (Miyuki 4222, Duracoat galvanized pewter)
- **1** e-shaped hook clasp (TierraCast)
- Fireline, 6 lb. test
- **2** beading needles, #13

Kits are available at enchantedbeadsbyjm.etsy.com

basics

- peyote stitch: flat odd-count, decreasing, zipping up or joining
- ending and adding thread
- attaching a stop bead

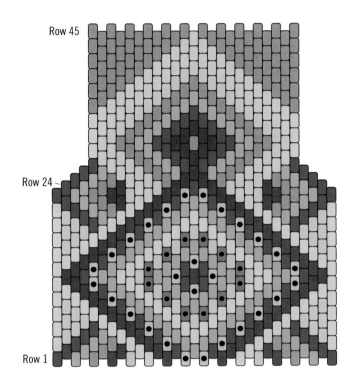

FIGURE 1

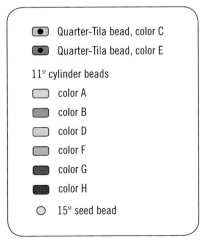

Quarter-Tila bead, color C

Quarter-Tila bead, color E

11º cylinder beads

color A

color B

color D

color F

color G

color H

15º seed bead

Stitch a flat peyote bracelet with 3D embellishments made by nestling cylinders and seed beads between Quarter-Tila beads.

When adding the Quarter-Tila beads, the open hole of the Quarter-Tila should be on the top surface of the band. When sewing through an existing Quarter-Tila, sew through the same hole as before, leaving the other hole open until directed.

BAND

1) On a comfortable length of thread, attach a stop bead, leaving a 6-in. (15 cm) tail. Pick up the beads for the first two rows: two color G cylinder beads, two color F cylinder beads, two color B cylinder beads, two color H cylinder beads, one color D cylinder bead, two color A cylinder beads, two Hs, one G, one color C Quarter-Tila bead, one F, one C, one G, two Hs, two As, one D, two Hs, two Bs, two Fs, and two Gs. These beads will shift to form rows 1 and 2 as the next row is added. Work in flat odd-count peyote stitch following the pattern (**figure 1**) or the word chart as follows, ending and adding thread as needed:

Row 3: 1A, 1G, 1F, 1B, 1A, 1H, 1C, 2Fs, 1C, 1H, 1A, 1B, 1F, 1G, 1A.

Row 4: 1D, 1G, 1F, 1A, 1H, 1G, 1F, 1A, 1F, 1G, 1H, 1A, 1F, 1G, 1D.

Row 5: 1A, 1D, 1G, 1A, 1H, 1C, 1F, 2A, 1F, 1C, 1H, 1A, 1G, 1D, 1A.

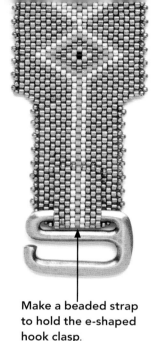

Make a beaded strap to hold the e-shaped hook clasp.

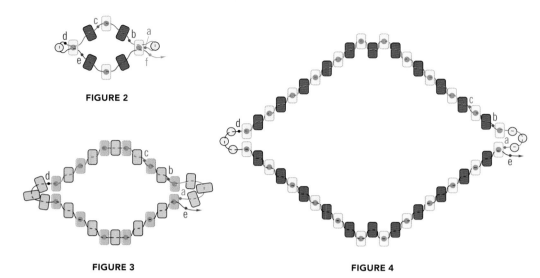

FIGURE 2

FIGURE 3

FIGURE 4

Row 6: 2D, 1A, 1H, 1G, 1F, 1A, 1D, 1A, 1F, 1G, 1H, 1A, 2D.

Row 7: 1A, 1D, 1A, 1H, 1C, 1F, 1A, two color E Quarter-Tila beads, 1A, 1F, 1C, 1H, 1A, 1D, 1A.

Row 8: 1D, 1A, 1H, 1G, 1F, 1A, 1D, 1F, 1D, 1A, 1F, 1G, 1H, 1A, 1D.

Row 9: 2A, 1H, 1C, 1F, 1A, 1E, 2F, 1E, 1A, 1F, 1C, 1H, 2A.

Row 10: 1A, 1H, 1G, 1F, 1A, 1D, 1F, 1C, 1F, 1D, 1A, 1F, 1G, 1H, 1A.

Row 11: 1A, 1H, 1C, 1F, 1A, 1E, 1F, 2G, 1F, 1E, 1A, 1F, 1C, 1H, 1A.

Row 12: 1H, 1G, 1F, 1A, 1D, 1F, 1C, 1H, 1C, 1F, 1D, 1A, 1F, 1G, 1H.

Row 13: Repeat Row 11.

Row 14: Repeat Row 10. Set aside the working thread.

2) Add 12 in. (30 cm) of thread in the beadwork, and exit the open hole of the C on the right side of the four center Cs, with your needle pointing toward the outside edge of the base **(figure 2, point a)** (only the four Cs are shown in the figure for clarity). Pick up a 15° seed bead, and sew back through the same hole of the C **(a–b)**.

3) Pick up a G, and sew through the open hole of the next C **(b–c)**. Repeat this stitch once, with the needle pointing toward the nearest edge of the band **(c–d)**. Pick up a 15°, and sew back through the same C **(d–e)**. Work two more stitches

using Gs as before **(e–f)**, and end this working thread and tail.

4) With the first working thread, continue in flat odd-count peyote:

Row 15: Repeat Row 9.

Row 16: Repeat Row 8.

Row 17: Repeat Row 7. Set aside the working thread.

5) Add 12 in. (30 cm) of thread to the beadwork, and exit the open hole of the lower of the two Es on the right side of the ring of Es, with the needle pointing toward the nearest edge of the band **(figure 3, point a)** (only the Es are shown in the figure for clarity).

6) Pick up three Ds, and sew through the open hole of the next E, with the needle pointing toward the opposite edge of the band, to form a picot **(a–b)**. Pick up a D, and sew through the open hole of the next E **(b–c)**. Repeat this last stitch four times **(c–d)**. Repeat all these stitches to complete the raised diamond shape **(d–e)**, and end this working thread and tail.

7) With the first working thread, continue in flat odd-count peyote:

Row 18: Repeat Row 6.

Row 19: Repeat Row 5.

Row 20: Repeat Row 4.

Row 21: Repeat Row 3.

Row 22: 1G, 1F, 1B, 1H, 1A, 1H, 1G, 1F, 1G, 1H, 1A, 1H, 1B, 1F, 1G.

Row 23: 1G, 1F, 1B, 1H, 1D, 1A, 1H, 2C, 1H, 1A, 1D, 1H, 1B, 1F, 1G.

8) Add 18 in. (46 cm) of thread to the beadwork, and exit the open hole of the lower of the two Cs on the right side of the ring of Cs, with the needle pointing toward the nearest edge of the band **(figure 4, point a)** (only the Cs are shown in the figure for clarity).

9) Pick up three 15°s, and sew through the open hole of the next C, with the needle pointing toward the opposite edge of the band, to form a picot **(a–b)**. Pick up a G, and sew through the open hole of the next C **(b–c)**. Repeat this last stitch 10 times **(c–d)**. Repeat all these stitches to complete the outer raised diamond shape **(d–e)**, and end this working thread and tail.

10) With the first working thread, continue in flat odd-count peyote:

Row 24: 1G, 1F, 1B, 1H, 1A, 1D, 1H, 1G, 1H, 1D, 1A, 1H, 1B, 1F, 1G. Make an odd-count turn after adding the last G, and continue through the last bead added to complete a decrease turn.

Row 25: 1G, 1F, 1B, 1A, 1D, 1B, 2H, 1B, 1D, 1A, 1B, 1F, 1G, decrease turn.

Row 26: 1G, 1F, 1A, 1D, 1B, 1F, 1H, 1F, 1B, 1D, 1A, 1F, 1G, decrease turn.

Row 27: 1G, 1A, 1D, 1B, 1F, 2G, 1F, 1B, 1D, 1A, 1G, decrease turn.

Row 28: 1A, 1D, 1B, 1F, 1G, 1H, 1G, 1F, 1B, 1D, 1A.

Row 29: 1A, 1D, 1B, 1F, 1G, 2H, 1G, 1F, 1B, 1D, 1A.

Row 30: 1D, 1B, 1F, 1G, 1H, 1B, 1H, 1G, 1F, 1B, 1D.

Row 31: Repeat Row 29.

Row 32: Repeat Row 28.

Row 33: 2A, 1D, 1B, 1F, 2G, 1F, 1B, 1D, 2A.

Row 34: 2A, 1D, 1B, 1F, 1G, 1F, 1B, 1D, 2A.

Row 35: 1B, 2A, 1D, 1B, 2F, 1B, 1D, 2A, 1B.

Row 36: 1B, 2A, 1D, 1B, 1F, 1B, 1D, 2A, 1B.

Row 37: 2B, 2A, 1D, 2B, 1D, 2A, 2B.

Row 38: 2B, 2A, 1D, 1B, 1D, 2A, 2B.

Row 39: 3B, 2A, 2D, 2A, 3B.

Row 40: 3B, 2A, 1D, 2A, 3B.

Row 41: 4B, 4A, 4B.

Row 42: 4B, 3A, 4B.

Row 43: 5B, 2A, 5B.

Row 44: 5B, 1A, 5B.

Row 45: 12B.

Row 46: Repeat Row 44.

Row 47: Repeat Row 43.

Row 48: 4B, 1A, 1D, 1A, 4B.

Row 49: 4B, 1A, 2D, 1A, 4B.

Row 50: 3B, 1A, 1D, 1G, 1D, 1A, 3B.

Row 51: 3B, 1A, 1D, 2G, 1D, 1A, 3B.

Row 52: 2B, 1A, 1D, 1G, 1F, 1G, 1D, 1A, 2B.

Row 53: 2B, 1A, 1D, 1G, 2F, 1G, 1D, 1A, 2B.

Row 54: 1B, 1A, 1D, 1G, 1F, 1H, 1F, 1G, 1D, 1A, 1B.

Row 55: Repeat Row 53.

Row 56: Repeat Row 52.

Row 57: Repeat Row 51.

Row 58: Repeat Row 50.

Row 59: Repeat Row 49.

Row 60: Repeat Row 48.

Row 61: Repeat Row 47.

Row 62: 5B, 1D, 5B.

Row 63: 5B, 2A, 5B.

Row 64: Repeat Row 62.

Row 65: Repeat Row 63.

Row 66: Repeat Row 62, decrease.

Row 67: 4B, 2A, 4B, decrease.

Row 68: 4B, 1D, 4B, decrease.

Row 69: 3B, 2A, 3B, decrease.

Row 70: 3B, 1D, 3B.

Row 71: 3B, 2A, 3B.

11) Alternate Rows 70 and 71 until you reach the desired length (figure 5). You want an even number of rows so the picots come out even during finishing.

12) To make the clasp strap, work in odd-count peyote stitch:

Strap, row 1: 15º seed bead, 2B, 1D, 2B, 15º, decrease turn.

Strap, row 2: 15º, 1B, 2A, 1B, 15º, decrease turn.

Strap, row 3: 2B, 1D, 2B.

Strap, row 4: 1B, 2A, 1B.

13) Repeat "Strap, rows 3–4" nine times.

FINISHING

1) Bend the strap to the back of the bracelet, and sew through an adjacent B where the end of the strap meets the band. Pick up a 15º, and work stitch-in-the-ditch to attach the end of the flap to the band. Pick up a 15º, and sew through the next B to end the connection (figure 6).

2) Sew through the adjacent B, the last 15º added, and the next B (figure 7, a–b). Pick up a 15º, and sew through the next cylinder (b–c). Repeat this stitch three times (c–d). Sew through the next 15º and B (d–e), and end the thread.

3) Finish the other end of the bracelet as a mirror image of this end. Before stitching the second strap in place, pass it through the closed end of the e-clasp.

4) Add a new thread at one end of the band, and exit the end edge B. Pick up three 15ºs, and sew down through the next edge B and up through the following edge B. Repeat to add picots of three 15ºs along all the straight edges (not the angled sides). Repeat along the other edge.

work it flat

No Quarter-Tila beads? Substitute 11º cylinder beads for the Quarter-Tilas for a flat version of the pattern.

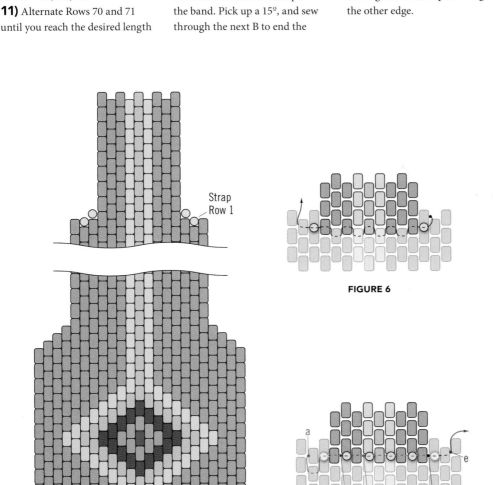

Strap Row 1

Row 46

FIGURE 5

FIGURE 6

a
b   c   d
e

FIGURE 7

Nautilus
earrings
by Graziella Malara

FIGURE 1

FIGURE 2

FIGURE 3

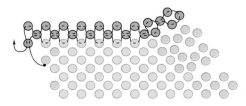

FIGURE 4

materials
blue earrings 1½ in. (3.8 cm)

- **40** 4 mm bicone crystals (Swarovski 5328, Caribbean blue opal)
- 15º seed beads
  - **3 g** color A (Toho PF558, permanent finish galvanized aluminum)
  - **3 g** color B (Miyuki 25, silver-lined capri blue)
- Fireline, 6 lb. test
- beading needles, #11 or #12
- **1** pair of earring findings
- **2** pairs of chainnose, bent-nose, and/or flatnose pliers

Find info for the alternate colorway at **FacetJewelry.com/resourceguide**

basics
- peyote stitch: flat odd-count
- ending and adding thread
- opening and closing jump rings

○ 15º seed bead, color A
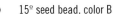
○ 15º seed bead, color B

⬡ 4 mm bicone crystal

Aquatic-inspired spirals of seed beads coil to create exotic earrings ready for beachwear.

NAUTILUS EARRING

1) On a comfortable length of thread, leave an 18-in. (46 cm) tail, and pick up one color A 15º seed bead, 15 color B 15º seed beads, and five As **(figure 1, a–b)**. These 21 beads will shift to form rows 1 and 2 as the next row is added. End and add thread as needed.

2) Work in flat odd-count peyote stitch as follows:

Row 3: Work 10 peyote stitches using two As and eight Bs **(b–c)**.

Row 4: Work seven peyote stitches using one B per stitch **(figure 2, a–b)**.

Tendril 2: Pick up six As, skip the last three As, and sew back through the next A **(b–c)**. Work one peyote stitch using an A **(c–d)**.

note The first "tendril" is the color A portion of the first row. The tendrils will be used to hold the edging crystals in place.

Row 5: Work seven peyote stitches using one B per stitch **(d–e)**.

Row 6: Pick up two As, and sew through the last B added in the previous row **(figure 3, a–b)**.

Work five peyote stitches using one B per stitch **(b–c)**.

Tendril 3: Pick up six As, skip the last three As, and sew back through the next A **(c–d)**. Work one peyote stitch using an A **(d–e)**.

Row 7: Work six peyote stitches using one B per stitch, sewing through an A after the last stitch **(e–f)**. Pick up one B, and sew through the next A **(f–g)**.

3) Repeat row 6, tendril 3, and row 7 **(figure 4)** 13 times for a total of 16 tendrils.

4) Repeat row 6 and tendril 3 once more **(figure 5, a–b)**. To finish the edge, work seven stitches with one A per stitch **(b–c)**.

5) Sew through the beadwork to exit the fourth bead added in the last

tip Because this project works a non-traditional peyote stitch along the edges, be sure to pay close attention as you turn to start a new row.

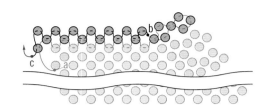

FIGURE 5

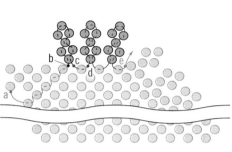

FIGURE 6

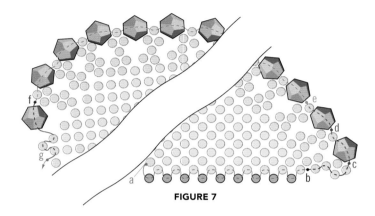

FIGURE 7

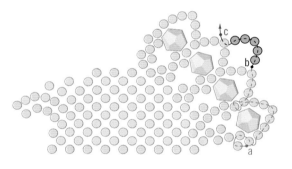

FIGURE 8

FIGURE 9

row (**figure 6, a–b**). Work a tendril as before (**b–c**), and sew through the next edge A (**c–d**). Repeat twice to add two more tendrils (**d–e**). Set the working thread aside.

6) With the tail, work nine peyote stitches with one A per stitch off of row 1 (**figure 7, a–b**), and then sew through the first tendril to exit the tip bead (**b–c**). Pick up a 4 mm bicone crystal, and sew through the tip bead of the next tendril (**c–d**). Repeat (**d–e**) until you have a total of 19 crystals (**e–f**). Pick up one more crystal, skip the next edge A, and sew through the following three As (**f–g**).

7) Sew through the beadwork to exit the tip bead of the nearest tendril (**figure 8, point a**). Pick up seven As, sew through the tip bead

of the next tendril, and sew back through the seventh bead just added (**a–b**).

8) Pick up six As, sew through the tip bead of the next tendril, and sew back through the last bead added (**b–c**). Repeat this step to add a loop of As around the outer edge of each of the remaining crystals.

9) To add a hanging loop, sew through the beadwork to exit the center A in the loop above the second-to-last crystal (**figure 9, a–b**). Pick up five As, and sew through the center A on the next loop (**b–c**). Sew through several more beads, and end the thread.

10) With the remaining thread, sew through the beadwork to exit an A on one end of the flat bottom edge, opposite the crystals. Zigzag

through the bottom edge beads to cinch the edge beads together. The beadwork should curve. When you reach the other end, form the beadwork into a spiral, with the end with the hanging loop on the outside and the end with the unembellished crystal near the center. Overlap the three beads on each end, and tack into this position, sewing through beads as needed. Gently fan the outer-edge beads outward. End the thread.

11) Open the loop of an ear wire, and attach it to the hanging loop.

12) Repeat steps 1–11 to make another earring. When forming the spiral, curve the beadwork in the opposite direction so the earrings are mirror images of each other.

Champagne bubble
necklace
by Diane Fitzgerald

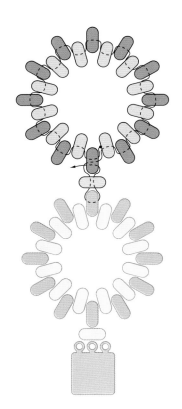

materials

three-strand necklace
19 in. (48 cm)

- 8º Demi beads
  - **16 g** color A (Toho 1F, crystal transparent matte)
  - **15 g** color B (Toho PF21, crystal silver-lined, permanent finish)
- **1** three-strand box clasp (Claspgarten, 14155/03)
- Fireline, 6 lb. test
- beading needle, #10
- disposable lighter or thread burner
- microcrystalline wax

three-ring earrings
1½ in. (3.8 cm)

- 8º Demi beads
  - **1 g** color A (Toho 1F, crystal transparent matte)
  - **1 g** color B (Toho PF21, crystal silver-lined, permanent finish)
- **2** 4 mm soldered jump rings
- **1** pair of ear wires
- **2** pairs of chainnose, bentnose, and/or flatnose pliers

triple dangle earrings
1¾ in. (4.4 cm)

- 8º Demi beads
  - **16 g** color A (Toho 1F, crystal transparent matte)
  - **15 g** color B (Toho PF21, crystal silver-lined, permanent finish)
- 11º hex-cut cylinder beads (Miyuka Delica DBC0035, galvanized silver)
- **2** 4 mm soldered jump rings
- **1** pair of ear wires
- **2** pairs of chainnose, bentnose, and/or flatnose pliers

basics

- peyote stitch: circular
- ending and adding thread
- opening and closing jump rings

This frothy concoction combines matte- and silver-lined Demi beads for a delicate and versatile project.

NECKLACE

1) Center a needle on 1 yd. (.9 m) of conditioned thread. Align the ends, and tie an overhand knot. Trim the tails 1 mm from the knot, and melt slightly with a lighter or thread burner to form a finished end.

2) Pick up 12 color A Demi beads. Push the beads to within 1 in. (2.5 cm) of the knot. Separate the strands between the beads and the knot. Pass the needle between the strands and then back through the last bead added. Pull tight to form a ring **(figure 1)**.

3) Working in circular peyote stitch, pick up a color B Demi bead, and sew through the following A. Repeat this stitch 11 times to complete the round, and step up through the first B added **(figure 2, a–b)**.

4) Pick up an A, and sew through the center clasp loop **(b–c)**. Sew back through the A and the B just exited, going in the same direction **(c–d)**. End your thread.

5) Repeat steps 1–4 33 times, but in step 4, attach the new ring to the B opposite the previous connection **(figure 3)**. After completing 34 rings, attach the last ring to the center loop on the other clasp half as in step 4.

6) Repeat steps 1–5 twice, but make one strand with a total of 33 components and one strand with a total of 35 components, attaching each strand to an open clasp loop.

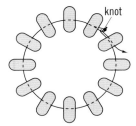

FIGURE 1

FIGURE 2

FIGURE 3

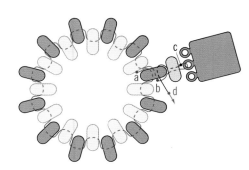

Option Convert this project from a three-strand necklace into one long strand without a clasp. This super-long necklace could be looped two or three times around your neck to suit your style.

EARRING OPTIONS

THREE-RING EARRINGS

1) Attach a soldered jump ring to an ear wire.
2) Work as in steps 1–4 of "Necklace" to make three connected rings, attaching an end ring to the soldered ring instead of a clasp **(figure 4)**.
3) Repeat to make a second earring.

TRIPLE DANGLE EARRINGS

1) Attach a soldered jump ring to an ear wire.
2) Work as in steps 1–3 of "Necklace."
3) Pick up an A, 21 11° hex-cut cylinder beads, and the soldered ring on the ear wire. Sew back through all the cylinders, and end the thread.
4) Work as in steps 1–3 of "Necklace," pick up an A and 15 cylinders, and sew through the last cylinder in the first strand and the soldered ring. Sew back through all the cylinders again, and end the thread.
5) Work as in step 4, but pick up 10 cylinders **(figure 5)**.
6) Repeat to make a second earring.

8° Demi bead, color A

8° Demi bead, color B

11° hex-cut cylinder bead

FIGURE 4

FIGURE 5

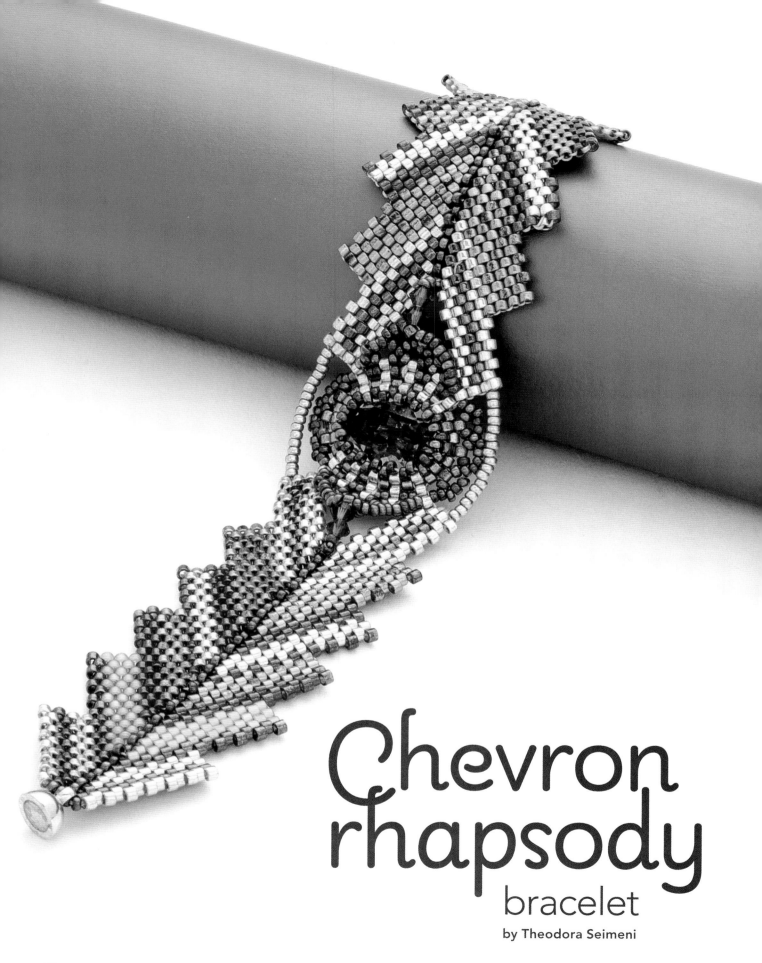

Chevron rhapsody
bracelet
by Theodora Seimeni

materials
bracelet 6¾ in. (17.1 cm)

- **1** 14 x 10 mm oval fancy stone (Swarovski 4120, crystal antique pink)
- **4** 3 mm bicone crystals (Swarovski, amethyst)
- 11º cylinder beads (Miyuki Delicas)
  - **3 g** color A (DB0040, copper plated)
  - **4 g** color B (DB0433, galvanized Champagne)
  - **2 g** color E (DB0461, galvanized tarnished copper)
  - **2 g** color F (DB0116, wine gold luster)
  - **1 g** color G (DB0622, dyed peach silver-lined alabaster)
- 15º seed beads (Miyuki)
  - **1 g** color C (462, metallic gold iris)
  - **1 g** color D (4204, Duracoat galvanized Champagne)
- **1** magnetic clasp
- Fireline, 6 lb. test
- beading needles, #11 or #12

basics

- peyote stitch: tubular, odd-count, stitch-in-the-ditch
- ladder stitch
- ending and adding thread

Create scores of peyote-stitched chevrons around a sparkling center stone for a dramatic composition.

BEZEL

1) On 4 ft. (1.2 m) of thread, pick up seven color A 11º cylinder beads, a repeating pattern of a color B 11º cylinder bead and an A four times, and then one more B. Pick up this 16-bead sequence again for a total of 32 beads. Leaving a 6-in. (15 cm) tail, tie the beads into a ring with a square knot **(figure 1, a–b)**, retrace the thread path twice (not shown in the figure for clarity), and sew through the first seven As added **(b–c)**. These beads will shift to form the first two rounds as the next round is added.

2) Working in tubular peyote stitch, work five stitches using Bs, three using As, five using Bs, and three using As, and step up through the first B added **(c–d)**.

3) Work a round using As, and step up **(d–e)**.

4) Work two rounds using color C 15º seed beads **(e–f)** using tight tension. After the last round, sew through the beadwork to exit a cylinder in the outer round of the bezel **(figure 2, point a)**. Place the 14 x 10 mm oval stone face up in the bezel, with the ends of the stone pointing toward the groups of seven As on the bezel, and gently form the bezel to come up around the stone. For clarity, just the two outer rounds of the bezel are shown, and the outer round is coming in toward the center of the stone.

5) Work two rounds with Cs to secure the stone **(a–b)**, and sew through the beadwork to exit the first A in a group of seven As (it will be in the second round of cylinders) **(figure 3, a–b)**.

6) Pick up an A, and sew through the next A in the same round **(b–c)**. Continue to work in stitch-in-the-ditch to work two more stitches using As, five using Bs, three using As, and five using Bs **(c–d)**. Make sure the stone stays in the correct position in the bezel. Sew through the beadwork in the bezel to exit the last B added, going in the same direction **(figure 4, point a)**.

7) Pick up three Cs, and sew through the next bead in the same round to form a picot **(a–b)**. Repeat this stitch three times **(b–c)**. Pick up two Cs, and sew through the following B. Repeat this last stitch three times **(c–d)**. Continue as before to work four stitches using three Cs and four stitches using two Cs to complete the round, and sew through the first two Cs added in this round to exit the center C of the first picot **(d–e)**.

8) Pick up three Cs, and sew through the center C in the next picot to form an end stitch **(e–f)**. Work another end stitch with four Cs and one more with three Cs, and sew through the following C **(f–g)**. Pick up a B, and sew through the

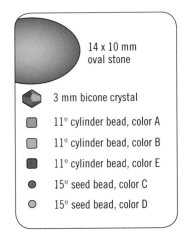

14 x 10 mm oval stone

3 mm bicone crystal

11º cylinder bead, color A

11º cylinder bead, color B

11º cylinder bead, color E

15º seed bead, color C

15º seed bead, color D

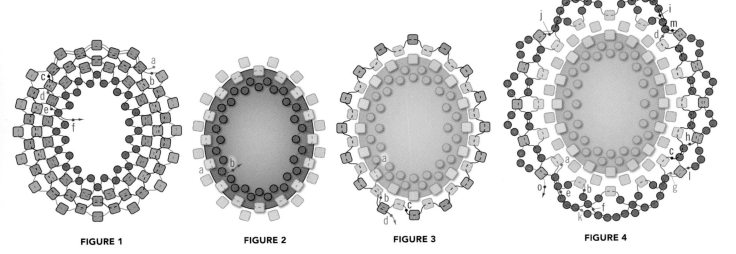

FIGURE 1

FIGURE 2

FIGURE 3

FIGURE 4

next two Cs to form a side stitch (**g–h**). Work four more side stitches (**h–i**). Work three end stitches using three Cs, four Cs, and three Cs, sewing through the following two Cs after the third end stitch (**i–j**). Work five side stitches with Bs, and then sew through the next three Cs (**j–k**).

9) Pick up a C, and sew through the four Cs of the next end stitch. Pick up a C, and continue through the following five Cs and B (**k–l**). Sewing through the Bs in the previous round, use Cs to add four three-bead picots (**l–m**), and then sew through the following five beads as shown (**m–n**). Work as before to add a C between the next two end stitches, and then use Cs to add three-bead picots between the Bs on the side. Do not continue through any Cs after the last stitch (**n–o**). Your thread should be exiting a B.

10) Sew under the nearest thread bridge and back through the B your thread is exiting and the next two Cs (**figure 5, a–b**).

11) Pick up four Cs, and sew through the center C in the next picot (**b–c**). Repeat this stitch twice, and sew through the next C and B (**c–d**). Sew under the nearest thread bridge, and continue back through the B your thread is exiting and the next five Cs (**d–e**).

12) Pick up four Cs, and sew through the two center Cs in the next picot. Repeat this stitch (**e–f**). Sew through the next three Cs and B, under the nearest thread bridge, and back through the B your thread is exiting and the next eight Cs (**f–g**).

13) Pick up a C, a B, and a C, skip the next four Cs, and sew through the following two Cs (**g–h**). Continue through the outer edge of the beadwork to exit the center C of the opposite picot (**h–i**).

14) Repeat steps 11–13 to embellish this side of the bezel, but do not sew through the outer edge beadwork in step 13. End the threads.

CHEVRON 1

1) Add 2 ft. (61 cm) of thread to the beadwork, exiting the B as shown with the needle pointing toward the side embellishment (**figure 6, point a**).

2) Work in rows as follows:

Rows 1–2: Pick up 11 Bs, a C, and 11 Bs, and sew through the corresponding B on the opposite end of the bezel as shown (**a–b**). These beads will shift to form rows 1 and 2 as the next row is added.

Row 3: Pick up a B, and sew through the last B added (**b–c**). Working in peyote stitch, work five stitches using Bs (**c–d**). Pick up a B, a C, and a B, and sew through the next B to form a point stitch (**d–e**). Work five peyote stitches using Bs, and sew through the B your thread exited at the start of this step (**e–f**). Pick up a B, sew through the B your thread is exiting, and continue through the B just added to work a ladder turn stitch (**f–g**).

Row 4: Work six stitches using color E cylinder beads, a point stitch with an E, a C, and an E, and six stitches using Es (**g–h**). Position the chevron so it sits slightly behind the beadwork on the side of the bezel as you work.

Row 5: Turn, and work a stitch with a B (**h–i**), and then work six stitches using Es, a point stitch with an E, a C, and E, six stitches using Es, and a ladder turn stitch using a B (**i–j**).

Row 6: Work seven stitches using Bs, a point stitch using a B, a C, and a B, and seven stitches using Bs (**j–k**).

Row 7: Work eight stitches using Bs, a point stitch using a B, a C, and a B, seven stitches using Bs, and a ladder turn stitch using a B (**k–l**). End the thread.

3) Repeat steps 1–2 on the other side of the bezel.

REMAINING CHEVRONS

1) Add a comfortable length of thread to the beadwork, exiting the fourth up-bead along the bottom edge of the first chevron, with the needle pointing toward the tip of the chevron (**figure 7, point a**).

2) Work in flat odd-count peyote as follows for the second chevron:

Row 1: Work five stitches using As, a point stitch using an A, a C, and an A, and five stitches using As (**a–b**). Sew through the beadwork to exit the last cylinder added (**b–c**).

Row 2: Work five stitches using As, a point stitch using an A, a C, and an A, and five stitches using As (**c–d**).

Row 3: Work six stitches using As, a point stitch using an A, a C, and an A, and five stitches using As. Work a ladder turn stitch as before using an A (**d–e**).

Row 4: Work six stitches using As, a point stitch using an A, a C, and an A, and six stitches using As (**e–f**).

Row 5: Work seven stitches using As, a point stitch using an A, a C, and an A, and six stitches using As. Work a ladder turn stitch using an A (**f–g**).

Row 6: Work seven stitches using As, a point stitch using an A, a C, and an A, and seven stitches using As (**g–h**).

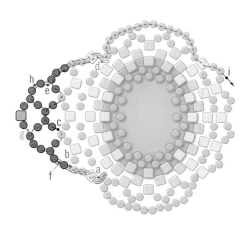

FIGURE 5

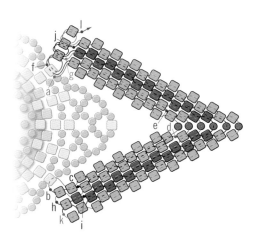

FIGURE 6

Row 7: Work eight stitches using As, a point stitch using an A, a C, and an A, and seven stitches using As. Work a ladder turn stitch using an A (**h–i**). Continue through the next six beads to exit the fourth up-bead to start the next chevron (**i–j**).

3) Work as in step 2 for the remaining chevrons with the following color changes for the cylinders, or devise your own color pattern. The C 15º on the tip remains the same for all the chevrons:

Chevron 3

Rows 1–3: Color F 11º cylinder beads

note Notice that in chevron 2, you worked the ladder turn on the top edge. In Chevron 3, the ladder turns will be on the bottom edge. These turns will change sides as each new chevron is added.

Rows 4–6: Bs

Row 7: Fs

Chevron 4

Rows 1–4: As

Rows 5–7: Fs

Chevron 5

Rows 1–5: Color G cylinder beads

Rows 6–7: Es. After adding row 7, sew through the beadwork to exit the fifth up-bead instead of the fourth.

Chevron 6

Rows 1–3: Bs

Rows 4–5: Es

Row 6: Work six stitches using Bs. Pick up a D, half of the clasp, and a D, and sew through the next E. Work six stitches using Bs.

Row 7: Work seven stitches using Bs, sewing through the D for the last stitch. Pick up a D, sew through the clasp loop, pick up a D, and continue through the next D. Work seven stitches using Bs. Sew through the beadwork and clasp connection to reinforce it, and end the thread.

4) Repeat steps 1–3 for the other side of the band.

EMBELLISHMENT

1) Add 1 yd. (.9 m) of thread to the beadwork, exiting the first C in a chevron attached to the bezel (**figure 8, point a**). Pick up two Cs and two 3 mm bicone crystals, and sew through the adjacent center A on the bezel (**a–b**). Sew back through the beads just added and the C your thread exited, going in the same direction (**b–c**). The beadwork on the edge of the bezel will be raised by the addition of these beads. Retrace the thread path (not shown in the figure for clarity), and sew through the beadwork to exit the top end B of chevron 1, exiting toward chevron 1 on the opposite band (**figure 9, point a**).

2) Pick up 17 Ds, and sew through the corresponding B on the opposite band (**a–b**). If needed, add additional Ds for the strand to curve slightly. Continue through the beadwork as shown to exit the adjacent B (**b–c**). Sew back through the beads just added and the next edge B on the first chevron (**c–d**). End this thread.

3) Add 12 in. (30 cm) of thread to the opposite side of the first chevron, and work as in steps 1–2 to complete the embellishment as a mirror image.

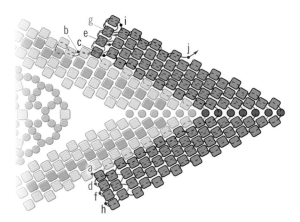

FIGURE 7

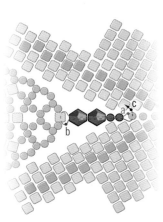

FIGURE 8

FIGURE 9

Lacy flower
earrings

by Magdalena Dec

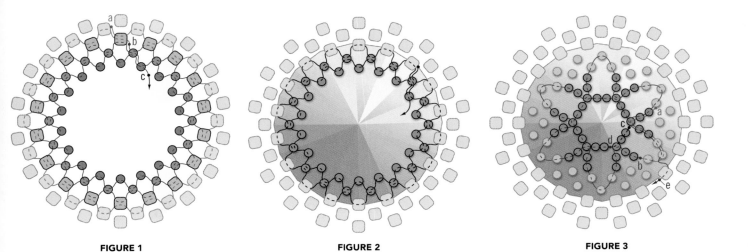

FIGURE 1   **FIGURE 2**   **FIGURE 3**

materials
green/blue earrings
2¼ in. (5.7 cm)

- **2** 14 mm rivoli (Swarovski, light Colorado topaz)
- **5 g** 11º seed beads (Toho PF567, permanent finish galvanized polaris)
- **1 g** cylinder beads (Miyuki DB168, opaque gray AB)
- 15º seed beads
  - **5 g** color A (Toho PF570, permanent finish galvanized mint green)
  - **1 g** color B (Toho PF567, permanent finish metallic polaris)
- **1** pair of earring findings
- Fireline, 6 lb. test
- beading needles, #11 or #12

Find info for the alternate colorway at
FacetJewelry.com/
resourceguide

basics

- square knot
- peyote stitch: tubular, flat odd-count
- stop bead
- ending and adding thread

These large and airy earrings are in full bloom and will be the highlight of your favorite summer outfit.

BEZEL

1) On 5 ft. (1.5 m) of thread, pick up 36 11º cylinder beads. Leaving a 6-in. (15 cm) tail, tie the beads into a ring with a square knot, and sew through the first few beads again. These beads will form the first two rounds as the next round is added.

2) Work a round of peyote stitch using cylinders, and step up through the first cylinder added **(figure 1, a–b)**.

3) Work one round using color A 15º seed beads and another round using color B 15º seed beads, stepping up at the end of each round **(b–c)**. Pull snug so the beadwork begins to cup.

4) Sew through the beadwork to exit a cylinder in the first round. Place the rivoli facedown into the beadwork. Stepping up at the end of each round, work two rounds using As **(figure 2)**.

5) Pick up five As, skip the next A in the previous round, and sew through the following three As as shown to form a picot **(figure 3, a–b)**. Repeat this stitch five times to complete the round, and step up through the first three As added **(b–c)**.

6) Pick up two As, and sew through the center A in the next picot **(c–d)**. Repeat this stitch five times to complete the round, retrace the thread path to tighten (not shown in the figure for clarity), and sew through the following four As and the adjacent cylinder as shown **(d–e)**. End the tail but not the working thread, and set the bezel aside.

PETALS

1) Attach a stop bead to 18 in. (46 cm) of thread, leaving a 6-in. (15 cm) tail. Pick up 37 As. These beads will form the first two rows as the next row is added.

2) Work in odd-count peyote stitch as follows using a tight tension:
Row 3: Work 18 stitches with one A per stitch **(figure 4, a–b)**. Pick up an A, and sew through the next three As as shown to exit the second-to-last A in row 3 **(b–c)**.
Row 4: Work two stitches using As, 12 stitches using 11º seed beads, and two stitches using As **(c–d)**. The beadwork will begin to curve. Sew through the beadwork as shown to exit the last A added **(figure 5, a–b)**.

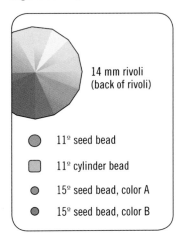

14 mm rivoli (back of rivoli)

- ○ 11º seed bead
- ☐ 11º cylinder bead
- ○ 15º seed bead, color A
- ● 15º seed bead, color B

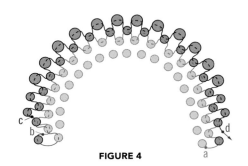

FIGURE 4

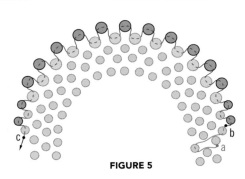

FIGURE 5

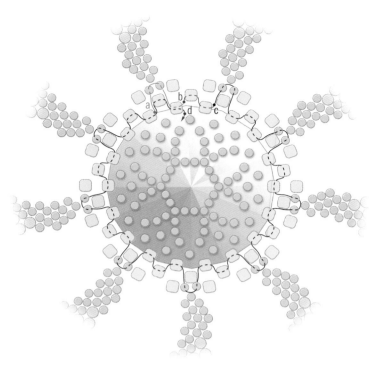

FIGURE 6

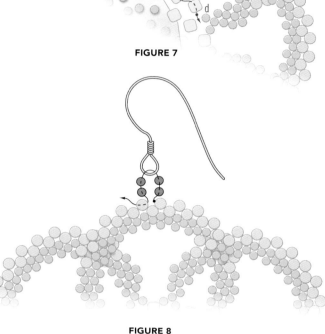

FIGURE 7

FIGURE 8

Row 5: Work two stitches using Bs, 11 using 11°s, and two using Bs (**b–c**). Remove the stop bead, and end the threads.

3) Repeat steps 1–2 to make a total of nine petals.

4) With the working thread from the bezel and the back facing up, sew up through the end A on the left arm of a petal, down through the adjacent end A, and through the next cylinder in the same round of the bezel (**figure 6, a–b**). Sew through the beadwork to exit the following cylinder in the same round (**b–c**). Repeat these stitches eight times to attach the left arms of the remaining petals (**c–d**). Sew through the beadwork as shown to exit the cylinder in the outer round of the bezel between the second and third petals (**figure 7, a–b**).

5) Attach the right arm of the first petal added as before, positioning this arm of the petal behind the left arm of the next petal (**b–c**). Sew through the beadwork to exit the following cylinder in the same round (**c–d**). Work as before to connect the remaining right arms of the petals, making sure each petal is positioned behind the next.

6) Sew through the beadwork to exit a bead where two petals overlap. Sew through an adjacent bead in the other petal, and back through a bead in the first petal to join the two layers together. Repeat this stitch two or three times between the two petals. Sew through the outer edge to reach the intersection of the next set of petals, and join them as before. Repeat to join the remaining petals.

7) After joining the last two petals, sew through the nearest petal to exit an outer edge 11° near the center of the petal. Pick up two Bs, the loop of an earring finding, and two Bs, and sew through the following 11° in the outer row (**figure 8**). Retrace the thread path several times, and end the thread.

8) Make a second earring but when attaching the petals, work in a counter-clockwise direction, and attach the right arms first instead of the left arms. When attaching the other arm of each petal, position the left arm behind the next petal going in a counter-clockwise direction, and attach as before. This makes a mirror image of the first earring.

Lotus blossom
pendant
by Lisa Kan

materials
turquoise pendant 3 in. (7.6 cm)

- **1** 14 mm crystal rivoli (Swarovski, crystal purple haze)
- **27** 3 x 6 mm CzechMates two-hole crescent beads (matte metallic bronze iris)
- **9** 2 mm fire-polished beads (transparent pink topaz luster)
- 11º seed beads
  - **15 g** color A (Toho 2634F, semi-glazed rainbow turquoise)
  - **1 g** color D (Toho 221, bronze)
  - **1 g** color E (Toho 85, purple iris)
- 15º seed beads
  - **1 g** color B (Toho 221, bronze)
  - **1 g** color C (Toho 85, purple iris)
  - **1 g** color F (Toho 2634F, semi-glazed rainbow turquoise)
- **1 g** 15º Charlotte beads (24k gold AB)
- Fireline, 6 lb. test
- beading needles, #12

Kits for all colors available at ariadesignstudio.com

Find info for the alternate colorways at **FacetJewelry.com/resourceguide**

basics
- cubic right-angle weave
- peyote stitch: tubular
- ending and adding thread
- square stitch

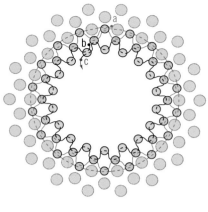

FIGURE 1

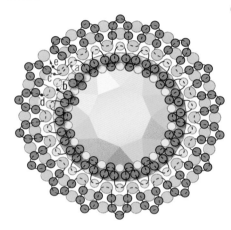

FIGURE 2

FIGURE 3

Embrace style with this stunning flower pendant with cupped seed bead petals.

BEZEL

How to pick up the crescent beads: With the tips of the crescent pointing toward you on your bead mat, pick up the crescent through the left hole (LH) or the right hole (RH).

1) On comfortable length of thread, work a cubic right-angle weave unit using 12 color A 11º seed beads, and leaving a 6-in. (15 cm) tail. Continue to work CRAW units to form a tube of 17 units. End and add thread throughout the beadwork as needed.

2) Using As, connect the ends of the CRAW tube to form a ring with a total of 18 CRAW units, making sure the tube is not twisted.

3) Sew through the beadwork to exit an inside-edge A with the needle pointing in a counter-clockwise direction **(figure 1, point a)**. For clarity, only one side of the CRAW base is shown in the following figures.

4) Work in tubular peyote stitch as follows, stepping up at the end of each round:

Round 1–2: Work two rounds using color B 15º seed beads, **(a–b)**.

Round 3: Work a round using 15º Charlottes **(b–c)**.

5) Sew through the beadwork to exit the corresponding A on the opposite inside edge of the CRAW base. Flip the beadwork over so the rows of peyote you just completed are on the bottom, and insert the rivoli faceup into the beadwork. Repeat step 4 to work the front of the bezel, and continue through the beadwork to exit a B in round 1 on the front of the bezel **(figure 2, point a)**. End the tail thread.

6) Pick up three Cs, skip the next inside edge A, and sew through the next B in the same round **(a–b)**. Repeat this stitch 17 times to complete the round, and sew through the following A on the top inside edge of the CRAW bezel **(b–c)**.

7) Pick up five Cs, and sew through the next A on the same inside edge **(c–d)**. Repeat this stitch 17 times to complete the round **(d–e)**. Sew through the beadwork to exit an A on the top outside edge of the CRAW bezel **(figure 3, point a)**. For clarity, the top bezel embellishment is not shown in the figure.

8) Pick up a color D 11º seed bead, and sew through the next A on the top outside edge **(a–b)**. Repeat this stitch 17 times to complete the round, and step up through the first D added **(b–c)**.

9) Pick up a B, a color E 11º seed

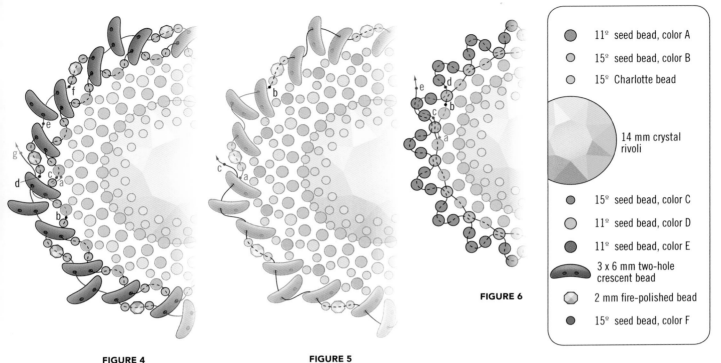

FIGURE 4

FIGURE 5

FIGURE 6

Legend (right panel):
- 11° seed bead, color A
- 15° seed bead, color B
- 15° Charlotte bead
- 14 mm crystal rivoli
- 15° seed bead, color C
- 11° seed bead, color D
- 11° seed bead, color E
- 3 x 6 mm two-hole crescent bead
- 2 mm fire-polished bead
- 15° seed bead, color F

bead, and a B, and sew through the next D to form a picot (**c–d**). Repeat this stitch 17 times to complete the round, and step up through the first B and E added (**d–e**).

10) Pick up B, a crescent bead (RH), and a B, and sew through the center E in the next picot (**figure 4, a–b**). Repeat this stitch 17 times to complete the round (**b–c**), retrace the thread path (not shown in the figure for clarity), sew through the first B and crescent added, and continue through the open hole of the same crescent (**c–d**). The crescents should curve inward toward the bezel with the open hole on top.

11) Pick up B, a 2 mm fire-polished bead, and a B, and sew through the open hole of the next crescent (**d–e**). Pick up a crescent (LH), and sew through the open hole of the following crescent (**e–f**). Repeat these stitches eight times to complete the round (**f–g**). The tips of the crescents just added should face up and the open hole should be on the outside.

12) Sew through the next B, 2 mm, B, adjacent top hole of the next crescent, open outside hole of the following crescent, and adjacent top hole of the next crescent (**figure 5, a–b**). Repeat this stitch eight times

to complete the round (**b–c**), and end the thread.

SMALL PETAL

1) Flip the beadwork over so the bottom of the bezel is facing up, and add a comfortable length of thread, exiting an A in the bottom outer edge of the CRAW bezel going clockwise (**figure 6, point a**).

2) Pick up a D, and sew through the next A on the bottom outside edge (**a–b**). Repeat this stitch 17 times to complete the round, and step up through the first D added (**b–c**).

3) Pick up three As, and sew through the next D to form a bezel picot (**c–d**). Repeat this stitch 17 times to complete the round, and sew through the first two As added (**d–e**).

4) Pick up 11 As, skip the last three beads added to form a picot, and sew back through the next A (**figure 7, a–b**). Working in peyote stitch, work four stitches using As, sewing through the center A in the bezel picot for the last stitch (**b–c**). Step up through the first A added in this step (**c–d**).

5) Work four peyote stitches with As (**d–e**). Pick up an A, and sew

through the center A of the end picot (**e–f**). Work five more stitches using As, sewing through the center A in the bezel picot after the last stitch, and step up through the first A added in this step (**f–g**).

6) Work four peyote stitches with As (**figure 8, a–b**). Pick up three color F 15° seed beads, skip the next end A, and sew through the following end A (**b–c**). Work four more stitches using As (**c–d**), and sew through the next five beads as shown to step up through the first A added (**d–e**).

7) Work three stitches using As, sew under the thread bridge between the next two As, and sew back through the A your thread just exited and the last A added (**e–f**). Tighten the thread slightly so the beadwork begins to cup toward the front of the bezel.

tip When stitching the small and large petals, use an even tension so beadwork only cups slightly and the edges are not over-curled.

8) Work two stitches using As, sew under the thread bridge between the next two As, and sew back

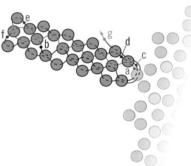

FIGURE 7

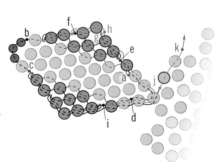

FIGURE 8

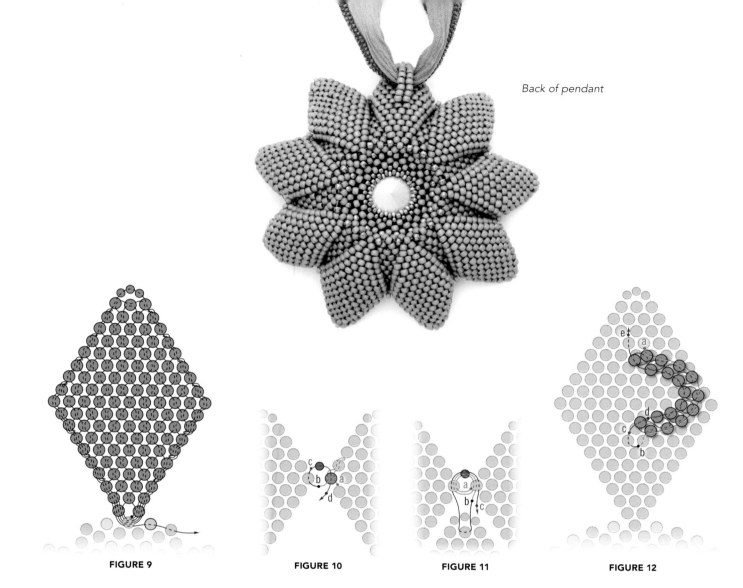

Back of pendant

FIGURE 9

FIGURE 10

FIGURE 11

FIGURE 12

through the A your thread just exited and the last A added (**f–g**).

9) Work one stitch using an A, sew under the thread bridge between the next two As, and sew back through the A your thread just exited and the last A added (**g–h**). Continue through the next nine beads as shown to exit the corresponding A on other side of the petal (**h–i**).

10) Work as in steps 7–9 to complete this side of the petal, and sew through the beadwork to exit the A in the bezel picot at the base of this petal (**i–j**). Pick up a D, and sew through the center A in the next bezel picot (**j–k**).

LARGE PETAL

Work as in "Small petal," but start with 19 As instead of 11 and work

additional rows on each side to complete the decreases (**figure 9**). For clarity, the small petal is not shown in the figure.

ADDITIONAL PETALS

1) Work another small petal, but in step 9 on the second side, exit the last A added (edge point) after securing it (**figure 10, a–b**). Position the small petals in front of the large petal. The large petal is not shown in the figure for clarity.

2) Sew through the corresponding edge point on the previous small petal (**b–c**), pick up an F, and sew through the A your thread exited at the start of this step, going in the same direction (**c–d**). Retrace the thread path several times, sew through the beadwork to exit the center A in the bezel picot, add the

D as before, and continue through the next bezel picot.

3) Work another large petal, but exit the last A added (edge point) on the second side after securing it. Make sure the large petals are positioned behind the small petals, and connect the two large petals in the same way as the small petals, retracing the thread path twice (**figure 11, a–b**). Sew through the end center A on the adjacent small petal, and continue through the side A on the first large petal, the new F, and the side A on the second large petal (**b–c**). Retrace this connection.

4) Sew through the beadwork to exit the center A in this bezel picot, pick up a D, and sew through the center A in the next bezel picot.

5) Continue adding and joining petals as before to complete the

round, and connect the last small and large petals to the first small and large petals as before.

BAIL

1) Sew through the beadwork to exit at **figure 12, point a** on a large petal.

2) Pick up nine As, skip the next three As in the peyote row, and sew down through the next A (**a–b**). Sew up through the adjacent bead (**b–c**).

3) Working in square stitch, pick up an A, sew through the last A added in the loop, and continue through the new A (**c–d**). Add eight more beads in square stitch, then sew through the A adjacent to the one the first loop of the bail is attached to (**d–e**). Retrace the thread path of the bail, and end the thread.

Climbing clematis
bracelet
by Michele Klous

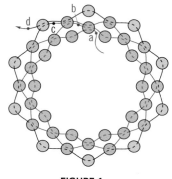

FIGURE 1

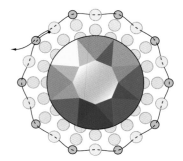

FIGURE 2

FIGURE 3

8 mm chaton

6 x 5 mm Nib-bit bead

3 x 5 mm Gekko bead

3.4 mm drop bead

8º seed bead

2 mm fire-polished bead

11º seed bead, color A

11º seed bead, color B

15º seed bead

FIGURE 4

FIGURE 5

materials

purple/blue bracelet, 7½ in. (19.1 cm)

- **8** 8 mm (SS39) chatons (azure blue)
- **32** 6 x 5 mm Nib-bit beads (black currant polychrome)
- **24** 3 x 5 mm Gekko beads (crystal apricot medium)
- **2 g** 3.4 mm drop beads (Miyuki 4512, opaque yellow Picasso)
- **2 g** 8º seed beads (Miyuki 4514, opaque turquoise blue Picasso)
- **14** 2 mm fire-polished beads (fern green mirror)
- 11º seed beads (Miyuki)
  - **4 g** color A (348, purple-lined light topaz luster)
  - **2 g** color B (1921, semi-frosted yellow-lined crystal)
- **2 g** 15º seed beads (Miyuki 354, chartreuse-lined green AB)
- **1** toggle clasp
- **2** 4 x 5 mm oval jump rings
- beading needle, #12
- Fireline, 6 lb. test
- **2** pairs of chainnose, flat-nose, and/or bentnose pliers

Find info for the alternate colorways at FacetJewelry.com/resourceguide

basics

- peyote stitch: tubular
- ending and adding thread

Welcome spring with a vibrant bracelet bursting with petal-like beads, crystal flower heads, and undulating green vines.

How to pick up Nib-Bit beads: With the wider flat bottom base nearest to you, sew through the top hole (TH) or the bottom hole (BH) per the instructions.

COMPONENTS

1) On 4 ft. (1.2 m) of thread, pick up 20 color A 11º seed beads, leaving a 6-in. (15 cm) tail. Sew through the beads again to form a ring (not shown in the figure for clarity), and continue through the first A (**figure 1, a–b**).

2) Working in tubular peyote, work 10 stitches using As, and step up through the first A added (**b–c**).

3) Work a round using color B 11º seed beads, and step up through the first B added (**c–d**).

4) Work a round using 15º seed beads. Place a chaton face up in the center of the beadwork, and step up through the first 15º added. (**figure 2**).

5) Pull the round of 15ºs snug to form a bezel around the chaton.

Retrace the thread path to reinforce the round (**figure 3**). (For clarity, just the top three rows of beads are shown.)

6) Turn the beadwork over so the back of the chaton is facing up, and sew through to exit an A in the inner round. Pick up a 15º, and sew through the next A in the same round, the following A in the adjacent round, and the next A in inner round (**figure 4, a–b**). Repeat this stitch four times to complete the round (**b–c**), and sew through the first 15º added and the next two As (**c–d**). Pull tight to secure the bezel.

7) Pick up a Nib-bit (TH), and sew through the next A in the same round (**figure 5, a–b**). Pull tight.

note Even after you pull tight, the Nib-bit will not stay snug at this time.

Repeat this stitch (**b–c**) until you have a total of four Nib-bits (**photo a**).

8) Pick up an 8º seed bead, and sew through the next A in the same round. Repeat this stitch five times, but after adding the last 8º, continue through the adjacent Nib-bit.

tip Retrace this entire round, going through all the beads: As, Nib-bits, and 8ºs. This will snug the beads in place (**photo b**).

9) Exiting the first Nib-bit added, pick up a B, and sew through the next Nib-bit. Repeat this stitch twice (**photo c**).

10) Pick up a 15º, and sew through the next 8º. Pick up a drop bead, and sew through the following 8º (**photo d**). Repeat this last stitch four times, and then pick up a 15º and sew through the next Nib-bit. Retrace the thread path through this round, exiting the first 8º (**photo e**).

11) Pick up an 8º, and sew through the next 8º.

note The newest 8º added sits on top of the drop bead and pushes it in for support.

Repeat this stitch four times, and then sew through the next 15º and Nib-bit (photo f). End the threads.

12) Repeat steps 1–11 seven times for a total of eight components.

ASSEMBLY

1) Place a component face up. Add 5 ft. (1.5 m) of thread to the bead-work, exiting the last 8º added below a drop bead at **figure 6, point a**.

2) Pick up six 15ºs, and sew through the open hole of the next Nib-bit (**a–b**).

3) Pick up a Gekko bead, and sew through the open hole of the next Nib-bit (**b–c**). Repeat this stitch twice (**c–d**).

4) Place a second component face up next to the first component, with the Nib-bits positioned on the opposite side. Pick up a B, and sew through the open hole of the next Nib-bit on the second component (**figure 7, a–b**). The Nib-bits on the connected components resemble an "S." Pick up a Gekko, and sew through the open hole of the next Nib-bit (**b–c**). Repeat this stitch twice (**c–d**).

5) Repeat step 4 to connect the remaining components.

6) Open two oval jump rings, and attach each one to half of the clasp.

7) Turn over the beadwork. Pick up six 15ºs and the jump ring attached to half of the clasp. Skip the next 15º and 8º and sew through the following 8º (**figure 8, a–b**). Sew through the next six 8ºs (**b–c**).

8) Pick up a 15º, an A, a 2 mm fire-polished bead, an A, and a 15º, and sew through the nearest Gekko on the next component (**c–d**). Sew through the next four beads (**d–e**). Pick up a 15º, an A, a 2 mm fire-polished bead, an A, and a 15º, skip the nearest three 8ºs on the next component, and sew through the following seven 8ºs (**e–f**). Repeat these stitches to connect all the components on both edges.

9) Sew through the beadwork to retrace the thread path of the con-nections, and reinforce both ends by sewing through the loop of 15ºs a couple of times.

10) Repeat step 6 to add the second half of the clasp to the loop of 15ºs on the opposite end.

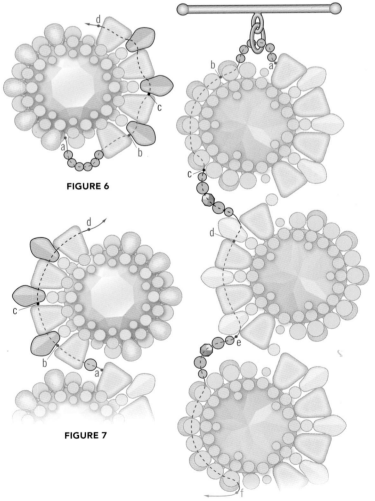

FIGURE 6

FIGURE 7

FIGURE 8

Icy Russian
ornament

Jane Danley Cruz

materials
ornament 2⅝ in. (6.7 cm)
- **1** 2⅝-in. (6.7 cm) glass ball ornament
- **20** 4 mm glass pearls (gray)
- **10** 4 mm Swarovski bicone crystals (crystal AB)
- **4 g** 11º seed beads color A (Miyuki 4201, Duracoat galvanized silver)
- **5 g** 11º Miyuki Delica cylinder beads in each of **3** colors
  - color B (DB0321, matte nickel plated)
  - color C (DB0630, dyed light smoke gray silver-lined alabaster)
  - color D (DBC0021, nickel plated, hex-cut)
- **1 g** 15º seed beads (Miyuki 190, nickel plated)
- Fireline, 6 lb. test
- beading needles, #11

basics
- diagonal peyote stitch
- attaching a stop bead
- ending and adding thread
- square knot

Embrace icy shades of silver and gray with this sparkling wintry ornament, featuring three sizes of Russian leaves suspended from a pearl collar.

MEDIUM LEAF
Side 1
1) Attach a stop bead in the center of 1 yd. (.9 m) of thread, and pick up one color A 11º seed bead, seven color B 11º cylinder beads, an A, and a B. Skip the last three beads, and sew back through the next B, with the needle pointing toward the tail (**figure 1, a–b**). Snug up the beads so the last A is at the end and the two adjacent Bs sit side by side.

2) Using Bs, work three peyote stitches (**b–c**). Your thread will be exiting the first A picked up in the previous step.

3) Using Bs, work three stitches in the opposite direction (**c–d**).

4) Work a decrease stitch to make the turn on this edge: Pick up an A and a B, and sew back through the last B added in the previous step (**d–e**). Work two peyote stitches using Bs (**e–f**).

5) Work an increase stitch to make the turn on this edge: Pick up a B, and A, and a B, skip the A, and sew back through the first B picked up in this step (**f–g**). Snug up the beads so the last A and B sit side by side. Position the A so it is on the side nearest the tail. As you work the remaining rows, keep the As to this edge. Work two peyote stitches using Bs (**g–h**).

6) Work as in steps 4–5 until you have seven As along each edge (**h–i**), and then work one more stitch using a B (**i–j**). End the working thread.

Side 2
1) Remove the stop bead, and attach a needle to the tail. With the thread exiting the end A, pick up a B, and sew through the next B in Side 1 (**figure 2, a–b**). Work two more peyote stitches using Bs (**b–c**).

2) Work as in steps 4–5 of "Side 1" until you have seven As along both edges (**c–d**). Work one more stitch using a B (**d–e**).

note The As at the start of Side 1 are shared with Side 2.

3) Join the two sides of the leaf: Sew through the beadwork to exit the outer B in the last increase (**figure 3, a–b**). Pick up a B, and sew through the corresponding end B on the outer edge of Side 1, with the needle pointing toward the point of the leaf (**b–c**). Snug up the beads. Turn, and sew through the adjacent A, with the needle pointing away from the beadwork (**c–d**). Pick up an A, and sew through the corresponding A on Side 2 (**d–e**). Retrace the thread path through the joining beads again. When you attach the leaf to the collar in the assembly steps, you will sew through the B added in this step.

4) There are three As along the upper inside-edge of the leaf. Sew through the beadwork to exit the edge A just before these three As (**figure 4, a–b**). Pick up an A, sew through the three upper-edge As (**b–c**), pick up an A, and sew through the next A on this edge (**c–d**). This will help the leaf keep its shape and prevent it

4 mm pearl

4 mm bicone crystal

11º seed bead, color A

11º cylinder bead, color B

15º seed bead

FIGURE 1

FIGURE 2

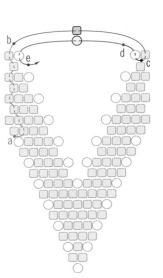

FIGURE 3

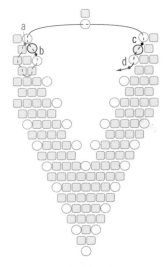

FIGURE 4

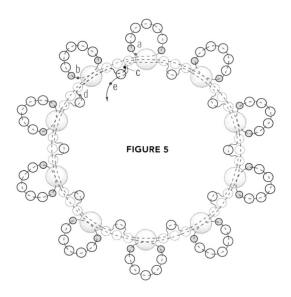

FIGURE 5

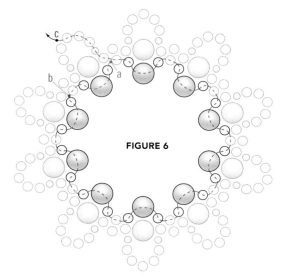

FIGURE 6

from collapsing. Sew through the beadwork, and end the threads.

5) Repeat all the previous steps to make two more leaves.

6) Make two more leaves using color C 11º cylinder beads in place of the Bs.

LARGE LEAF

1) Work as in "Medium Leaf," but repeat steps 4–5 until there are a total of nine As along each edge for both Side 1 and Side 2.

2) Make two large leaves using Cs instead of Bs.

3) Make two large leaves using color D hex-cut beads instead of Bs.

SMALL LEAF

1) Work as in "Medium Leaf" using Cs instead of Bs and with the following changes:

• **Step 1:** Pick up five Cs instead of seven Bs.

• **Step 2:** Work two peyote stitches instead of three.

• **Step 3:** Work two peyote stitches instead of three.

• **Step 4:** Work one peyote stitch instead of two.

• **Step 5:** Work one peyote stitch instead of two.

• **Step 6:** Work until you have five As along each edge, then work a final peyote stitch.

2) Work Side 2 as you worked Side 1, but do not end the tail

thread. Later, you will use the tail to connect the small leaf to the tip of a medium leaf.

3) Make two more small leaves using Cs.

4) Make two small leaves using Ds.

COLLAR

1) On 1 yd. (.9 m) of thread and leaving a 6-in. (15 cm) tail, pick up a repeating pattern of a 4 mm glass pearl and three As 10 times. Tie the ends together with a square knot to form a ring. Sew through the next few beads, and pull the thread tight to hide the knot. Continue through the beads to exit the nearest pearl.

2) Pick up a 15º seed bead, five As, and a 15º, sew through the same pearl, going in the same direction, and continue through the next three As and the following pearl (figure 5, a–b). The new beads will form a loop around the pearl. Repeat this stitch nine times to complete the round, and sew through the next A (b–c).

3) Pick up an A, skip the next A in the original ring, and sew through the following A, pearl, and A (c–d). Repeat this stitch nine times to complete the round, and step up through the first A picked up in this round (d–e).

4) Pick up an A, a pearl, and an A, and sew through the next A added

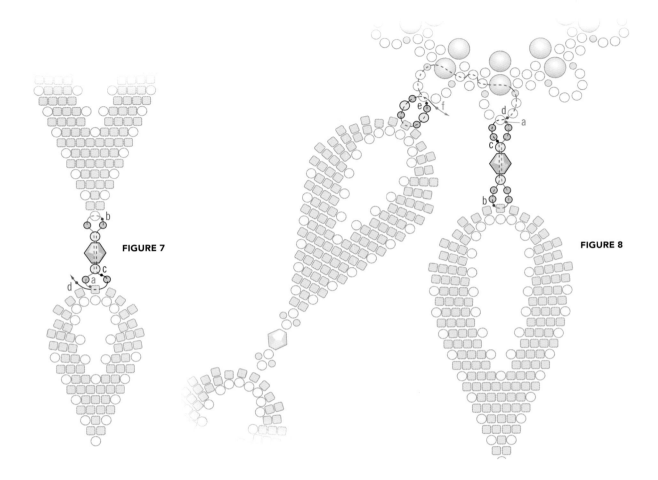

FIGURE 7

FIGURE 8

in the previous round (**figure 6, a–b**). Repeat this stitch nine times to complete the round, and sew through the beadwork to exit the third A in the seven-bead loop around a pearl (**b–c**). End the tail but not the working thread.

MEDIUM LEAF/SMALL LEAF COMPONENT

1) Attach a needle to the tail thread of a small leaf, and exiting the center cylinder at the base of the leaf, pick up a 15º, an A, a 4 mm bicone crystal, an A, and a 15º, and sew through the A at the tip of a medium leaf of your choice (**figure 7, a–b**). Pick up a 15º,

and sew back through the last A, crystal, and A (**b–c**). Pick up a 15º, and sew through the cylinder bead your thread exited at the start of this step (**c–d**). Retrace the thread path through the join several times, and end the thread.

2) Work as in step 1 to attach the remaining small leaves to the tips of the medium leaves.

ASSEMBLY

1) Attach a needle on the working thread of the collar — the thread should be exiting the center A in the loop around a pearl.

2) Attach a large leaf: Pick up two 15ºs, an A, a crystal, an A, and two

15ºs, and sew through the center cylinder at the base of a large leaf — this is the joining cylinder (**figure 8, a–b**). Pick up two 15ºs, and sew back through the A, crystal, and A just added (**b–c**). Pick up two 15ºs, and sew through the A in the loop your thread exited at the start of this step (**c–d**). Retrace the thread path through all the beads in this step (not shown in the figure for clarity), and then sew through the beadwork in the collar to exit the center A in the loop around the next pearl (**d–e**).

3) Attach a medium leaf/small leaf component: Pick up a 15º, an A, and a 15º, and sew through the

joining cylinder at the base of a medium leaf. Pick up a 15º, an A, and a 15º, and sew through the A your thread exited at the start of this step (**e–f**). Retrace the thread path through the beads added in this step and sew through the beadwork to exit the center A in the loop around the next pearl.

4) Continue to work as in steps 2–3 to complete the round. End the threads.

Crowned empress
bracelet

by Theodora Seimeni

materials
bracelet 6½ in. (16.5 cm)

- **1** 14 mm rivoli (Swarovski, crystal lilac shadow)
- crystal pearls (Swarovski)
  - **2** 6 mm (burgundy)
  - **4** 5 mm (burgundy)
  - **4** 4 mm, color A (burgundy)
  - **6** 4 mm, color B (platinum)
- **4** 4 mm bicone crystals (Swarovski, amethyst AB)
- **1 g** color I 11º seed beads (Miyuki 4220, Duracoat galvanized eggplant)
- 11º cylinder beads (Miyuki Delicas)
  - **3 g** color C (DB0038, palladium plated)
  - **4 g** color D (DB1850, Duracoat galvanized eggplant)
- 15º seed beads
  - **1 g** color E (Toho 222, dark bronze)
  - **1 g** color F (Miyuki 401F, black matte)
  - **18** color H (Miyuki 4202F, Duracoat galvanized matte gold)
  - **1 g** color J (Miyuki 194, palladium plated)
- **1 g** 15º cylinder beads, color G (Miyuki Delica DBS310, black matte)
- **1** 3-strand tube clasp
- nylon beading thread, size B, or Fireline, 6 lb. test
- beading needles, size #11 or #12

basics
- attaching a stop bead
- peyote stitch: flat odd-count, tubular
- ending and adding thread
- square knot

Feel like royalty when you wear this delicate but stately bracelet made with Delicas, pearls, and crystals.

END UNITS

1) On 5 ft. (1.5 m) of thread, attach a stop bead, leaving a 12-in. (30 cm) tail. Pick up a color C 11º cylinder bead, two color D 11º cylinder beads, 13 Cs, two Ds, and a C (**figure 1, a–b**). These beads will shift to form rows 1 and 2 as the next row is added. Work in flat odd-count peyote stitch as follows to make an end unit, referring to **figure 1**:

Row 3: one C, one D, six Cs, one D, and one C
Row 4: one D, seven Cs, and one D
Rows 5–8: Repeat rows 3–4 two times
Row 9: one C, eight Ds, and one C
Row 10: nine Ds
Rows 11–16: Repeat rows 9–10 three times
Rows 17–24: Repeat rows 3–4 four times

sizing note To increase or decrease the length of the bracelet, add or omit rows on each end unit. Fourteen rows equals ½ in. (1.3 cm), so to increase your bracelet by ½ in. (1.3 cm), add seven rows to each end unit. Be sure to end with an even number of rows.

2) Sew through the beadwork to exit the fifth (center) up-bead in the last row (**c–d**). Do not end the threads.
3) Repeat steps 1–2 to make another end unit.

BAND STRIPS

1) Attach a comfortable length of thread to an end unit, exiting an edge C in the second-to-last row (**figure 2, point a**).
2) Working in flat even-count peyote stitch, work a stitch with a C and one with a D (**a–b**). Repeat this

stitch to add a total of 59 new Cs along the outside edge and 58 along the inside edge (**b–c**). Sew through the last three rows to reinforce, and exit the end outer-edge C with the needle pointing toward the opposite edge.

3) Work as in steps 1–2 to make another strip on the opposite edge of the end unit. Set the end units aside.

BEZEL

1) On 4 ft. (1.2 m) of thread, pick up 36 Ds. Leaving a 20-in. (51 cm) tail, tie the beads into a ring with a square knot, and sew through all the beads again. These beads will shift to form the first two rounds as the next round is added.

2) Work a round of tubular peyote stitch using Ds (**figure 3, a–b**), and a round using color E 15º seed beads (**b–c**), stepping up after each

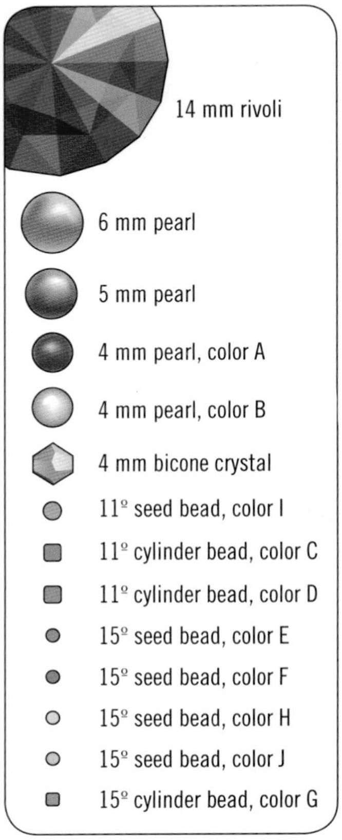

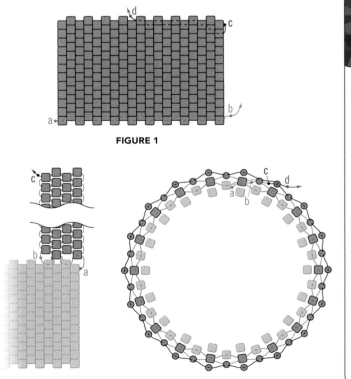

FIGURE 1

FIGURE 2

FIGURE 3

14 mm rivoli

6 mm pearl

5 mm pearl

4 mm pearl, color A

4 mm pearl, color B

4 mm bicone crystal

11º seed bead, color I

11º cylinder bead, color C

11º cylinder bead, color D

15º seed bead, color E

15º seed bead, color F

15º seed bead, color H

15º seed bead, color J

15º cylinder bead, color G

round. Use tight tension so the beadwork begins to cup.

3) Work a round using one bead per stitch in a repeating pattern of a color F 15º seed bead and two Es, six times, and step up **(c–d)**. Set the working thread aside, and attach a needle to the tail. With the tail, sew through the next D in round 1 **(figure 4, point a)**.

4) Place the 14 mm rivoli face up in the beadwork. Work a round using color G 15º cylinder beads **(a–b)** (only round 1 of the Ds are shown in the figure for clarity), and a round using Es **(b–c)**. Retrace the thread path using tight tension (not shown in the figure for clarity), and sew through the beadwork to exit a D in round 1 **(figure 5, a–b)**.

5) Pick up a color H 15º seed bead, and sew through the next D in round 1 **(b–c)**. Repeat this stitch

17 times to complete the round **(c–d)**, and end the tail.

6) Flip the bezel over to the back, and with the working thread exiting an F, pick up two Es, an F, and two Es, and sew through the following F **(figure 6, a–b)**. Repeat this stitch five times, and sew through the first three beads added **(b–c)**.

7) Pick up an E, an F, and an E, and sew through the next center F in the previous round **(c–d)**. Repeat this stitch five times, and sew through the first two beads added **(d–e)**.

8) Pick up an E, and sew through the next center F in the previous round **(e–f)**. Repeat this stitch five times, and sew through the first E added **(f–g)**. Without adding any beads, sew through the Es added in this round twice using tight tension, and end this thread.

BEZEL EMBELLISHMENT

1) On 2 yd. (1.8 m) of thread, sew through a D in the center round of Ds along the edge of the bezel, leaving a 20-in. (51 cm) tail.

2) Pick up a color I 11º seed bead, and sew through the next D in the same round **(figure 7, a–b)**. Work two more stitches, one using a D, and one using an I **(b–c)**. These three beads will be row 1 for the top tab.

3) Continue working in stitch-in-the-ditch with the following beads to complete the round: two Es, two Ds (these two beads will be row 1 for the left-side tab), two Es, one I, one D, one I (these three beads will be row 1 for the bottom tab), two Es, two Ds (these two beads will be row 1 for the right-side tab), and two Es. Step up through the first I added **(c–d)**.

4) Work two stitches using Ds

(d–e). Using Ds, work eight rows of flat odd-count peyote stitch, using tight tension for a total of 10 rows in this tab. Each edge should have one I and four Ds.

5) Sew through the beadwork as shown to exit the first D added in row 10 **(figure 8, a–b)**. Pick up a D, and sew through the next two Ds **(b–c)**.

6) Pick up three Es, and sew through the next two edge Ds **(c–d)**. Repeat this stitch once more, exiting an I **(d–e)**.

7) Pick up four Es, and sew through the next E along the edge of the bezel **(e–f)**. Pick up an E, and continue through the next E **(f–g)**.

8) Work three stitches using an I, a D, and an I to complete row 2 of the left-side tab **(g–h)**.

9) Pick up an E, and continue through the next E. Pick up four Es, and sew through the next I **(h–i)**.

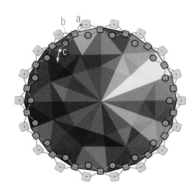

FIGURE 4

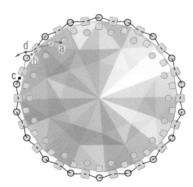

FIGURE 5

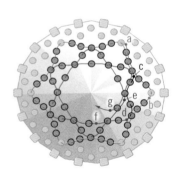

FIGURE 6

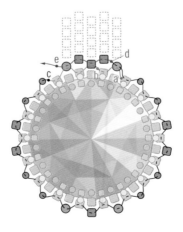

FIGURE 7

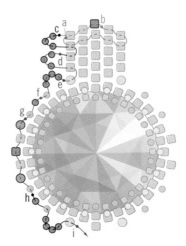

FIGURE 8

10) Repeat steps 4–9 to work the bottom tab and row 2 of the right-side tab. Sew through the next edge D in the top tab **(figure 9, point a)**.

11) Pick up three Es, and sew through the next two edge Ds to make a picot. Make another picot, sewing through two more Ds to exit the tip D on this tab **(a–b)**.

12) Using three Es, make a picot at the tip, sewing through the same D **(b–c)**. Retrace the thread path twice (not shown in the figure for clarity), and continue through the beads as shown **(c–d)**.

13) Pick up two Es, skip the next E, and sew through the following I **(d–e)**. Repeat steps 4–6 to add the left-side tab. Your thread should be exiting the I at **point f.**

14) Pick up two Es, skip the next E, and sew through the following E **(f–g)**. Sew through the beads as shown to exit the next edge D in the bottom tab **(g–h)**.

15) Repeat steps 11–12 **(h–i)**. Pick up two Es, skip the next E, and sew through the following I **(i–j)**. Add the right-side tab as in steps 4–6. Your thread should be exiting the I at **point k.**

16) Pick up two Es, skip the next E, and sew through the following E **(k–l)**.

17) Sew through the beadwork to the left-side tab, exiting the first edge D on the unembellished edge. Work as before to add the edge and tip picots. Sew through the beadwork to the right-side tab, and embellish as before. End the working thread.

18) Attach a needle to the tail, and sew through the beadwork to the nearest tab, exiting the E in **figure 10, point a.** Pick up an E, a 4 mm bicone crystal, two Es, a G, two Es, a G, two Es, a G, and an E, and

sew through the corresponding E in the picot on the next tab to form an arch **(a–b)**. Sew through the beadwork to exit the corresponding E in the picot on the opposite edge of the same tab **(b–c)**. Pick up an E, a G, two Es, a G, two Es, a G, two Es, a bicone, and an E, and sew through the corresponding E in the picot on the next tab **(c–d)**. Repeat these stitches once, and sew through the first E and bicone added **(d–e)**.

19) Work five peyote stitches using Es, and sew through the E in the picot this arch is attached to on the next tab **(e–f)**. Sew through the

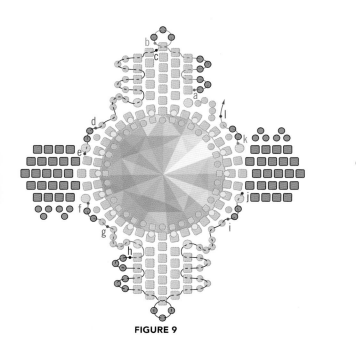

FIGURE 9

FIGURE 10

beadwork to the opposite edge and exit the next two Es (f–g). Work five peyote stitches using Es, and sew through the next bicone and two Es (g–h). Sew through the beadwork to exit the bicone in the next arch (h–i), and repeat these stitches to complete the round (i–j). End the tail.

ASSEMBLY

1) Place the center component face up on your bead mat, with the tabs with the crystals at the top and bottom. With the end unit with the strips attached, weave the bottom strip over the bottom-right arch, under the bottom tab, and over the bottom-left arch (photo a). With the top strip, weave the strip over the top-right arch, under the top tab, and over the top-left arch (photo b).

2) Align the other end unit with the ends of the strips as shown in figure 11. With the working thread from the top strip, sew through the adjacent edge C in the end unit and the C your thread exited at the start of this step, going in the same direction (a–b). Zip the remainder of the strip to the end unit (b–c). Sew through the adjacent C in the strip, and the same C in the end unit your thread just exited (c–d). End this thread. Repeat these stitches to attach the bottom strip.

3) With the working thread from the end unit exiting the center up-bead, pick up an E, a color A 4 mm pearl, an E, an A, an E, a 5 mm pearl, an E, a 5 mm pearl,

an E, and a 6 mm pearl, and sew through the center bead in the picot on the end of the adjacent tab (figure 12, a–b). Sew back through the beads just added, and the C your thread exited at the start of this step, going in the same direction (b–c). Retrace the thread path twice, and end this thread.

note If needed, add more Es to the pearl connection or replace a smaller size pearl with a larger one. Make the same changes for the connection on the other side.

4) With the working thread from the other end unit, repeat step 3 to attach the other side tab to the other end unit.

CLASP

1) Remove the stop bead from an end unit. With the tail thread, sew through the beadwork as shown to exit the third up-bead in row 1 (figure 13, a–b). Pick up a color B 4 mm pearl, three color J 15º seed beads, an end clasp loop, and three Js, and sew back through the B and the next up-bead in row 1 (b–c). Sew through the next two beads to exit the following up-bead (c–d). Repeat these stitches to connect the remaining clasp loops (d–e). Sew through the beadwork, retrace the thread path of the clasp connection, and end this thread.

2) With the tail thread from the other end unit, repeat step 1 to add the other half of the clasp.

a

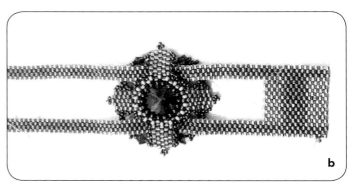
b

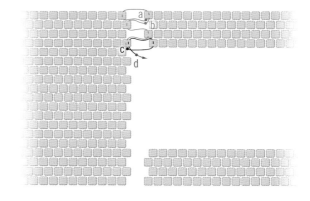

FIGURE 11

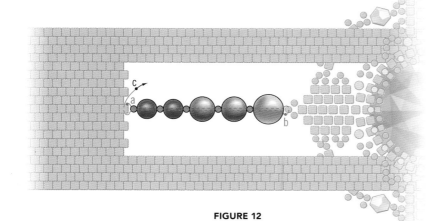

FIGURE 12

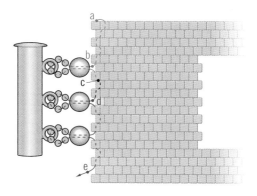

FIGURE 13

Ribbons and bows
bracelet
by Ellie Hamlett

materials
bronze bracelet 6½ in. (16.5 cm)

- **12** 9 x 17 mm carrier beads (green red luster)
- **22** 6 mm Kheops par Puca beads (light matte gold)
- **11** 4 mm fire-polished beads (ivory mercury)
- **17 g** 3 mm cube beads (Miyuki 457, metallic dark bronze)
- **2 g** 8º seed beads (Miyuki 457, metallic dark bronze)
- **4 g** 11º seed beads (Miyuki 457, metallic dark bronze)
- **1 g** 15º seed beads (Miyuki 1882, dark topaz gold luster)
- **6** 6 mm jump rings
- **1** 3-strand tube clasp
- Fireline, 6 or 8 lb. test
- beading needles, #11 or #12
- **2** pairs of chainnose, flatnose, and/or bentnose pliers

Kits are available at thebuffalobeadgallery.com

Find info for the alternate colorway at **FacetJewelry.com/resourceguide**

basics

- peyote stitch: flat even count
- crossweave
- attaching a stop bead
- ending and adding thread
- opening and closing loops and jump rings

Craft a simple peyote band with cube beads and dress it up with a ribbon of carrier beads interspersed with tiny beaded bows.

BASE

On a comfortable length of thread, attach a stop bead, leaving a 6-in. (15 cm) tail. Pick up six 3 mm cube beads. Working in flat even-count peyote and ending and adding thread as needed, stitch a six-bead wide band to the desired length, making sure the number of cubes on each edge of the base is divisible by four. Allow ½ in. (1.3 cm) for the clasp. Work four more rows so there are two additional cubes on each edge. Note: Eight rows (or four rows on each edge) equals ½ in. (1.3 cm).

EDGE PICOT EMBELLISHMENT

1) Pick up three 11º seed beads and sew through the next up-bead. Repeat this stitch two times to complete the row **(figure 1, a–b)**.
2) Pick up three 11ºs, and sew through the adjacent edge cube and the next edge cube to form a picot **(b–c)**. Repeat this stitch to add picots for the remainder of this side.
3) Sew through the base to exit the end edge cube on the opposite side **(figure 2, a–b)**. Repeat step 1, sewing through the end cube for the last stitch, with the needle pointing toward the opposite edge **(b–c)**. Sew through the beadwork to exit the end cube on the opposite edge **(c–d)**.
4) Repeat step 2 to add picots along this edge, and end the threads.

EMBELLISHMENT

1) Position your beadwork vertically on your bead mat with an up-bead in the lower right, and attach a needle to each end of a comfortable length of thread. Sew through the center four cubes, and center your thread. With each needle, sew through the adjacent cube in the same vertical row, with the needles pointing toward the center of the beadwork **(figure 3, point a and aa)**.
2) With one needle, pick up a carrier bead, skip two cubes in the same vertical row, and sew through the next cube, with the needle pointing toward the nearest edge **(a–b)**. Continue through the next cube in the same row, sewing toward the center of the beadwork **(b–c)**. Repeat with the other needle, sewing through the open hole of the carrier **(aa–bb)**. Repeat these stitches for the remainder of the base. The carriers will sit at a slight angle until the next step is complete.
3) On each needle, pick up an 8º seed bead, and sew through the adjacent hole of the last carrier added **(figure 4, a–b and aa–bb)**.
4) Pick up an 8º, an 11º and an 8º, and sew through the corresponding hole of the next carrier **(b–c and bb–cc)**. Repeat this stitch to add beads between the remaining carriers. The beadwork will begin to curve.
5) With each needle, pick up an 8º, and sew through the end two cubes as shown, with the needle going toward the outside edge **(figure 5, a–b and aa–bb)**. Continue to sew through the beadwork as shown to exit the third 11º on the second set of edge picots on each edge **(b–c and bb–cc)**.

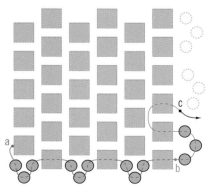

FIGURE 1

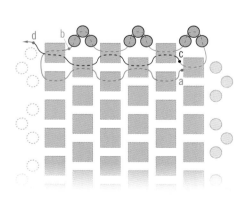

FIGURE 2

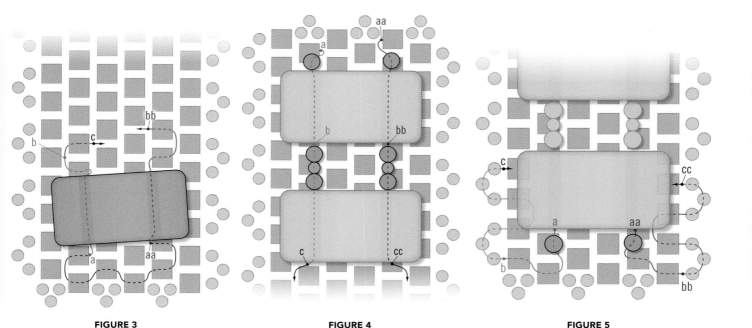

FIGURE 3   **FIGURE 4**   **FIGURE 5**

6) With each needle, pick up an 11º, a 15º seed bead, a Kheops, and four 15ºs **(figure 6, a–b and aa–bb)**. With one needle, pick up an 11º, a 4 mm fire-polished bead, and an 11º, and cross the other needle through the three beads just added **(b–c and bb–cc)**.

7) With each needle, pick up four 15ºs, and sew through the open hole of the adjacent Kheops **(c–d and cc–dd)**. Pick up a 15º and an 11º, skip the next picot, and sew through the beads in the following picot **(d–e and dd–ee)**.

8) Repeat steps 6–7 for the remainder of the base.

9) Sew through the beadwork to reinforce the picots on the end of the base, and end the working thread. Repeat with the tail.

10) Open a jump ring, and attach the loop on one half of the clasp to a picot on the end of the bracelet. Repeat to attach the other two loops of the clasp to the other picots. Repeat to attach the other half of the clasp to the other end of the bracelet.

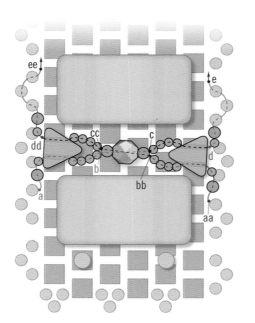

FIGURE 6

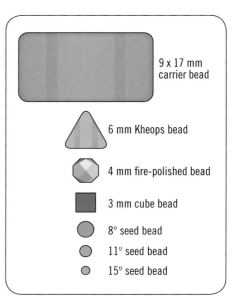

9 x 17 mm carrier bead

6 mm Kheops bead

4 mm fire-polished bead

3 mm cube bead

8º seed bead

11º seed bead

15º seed bead

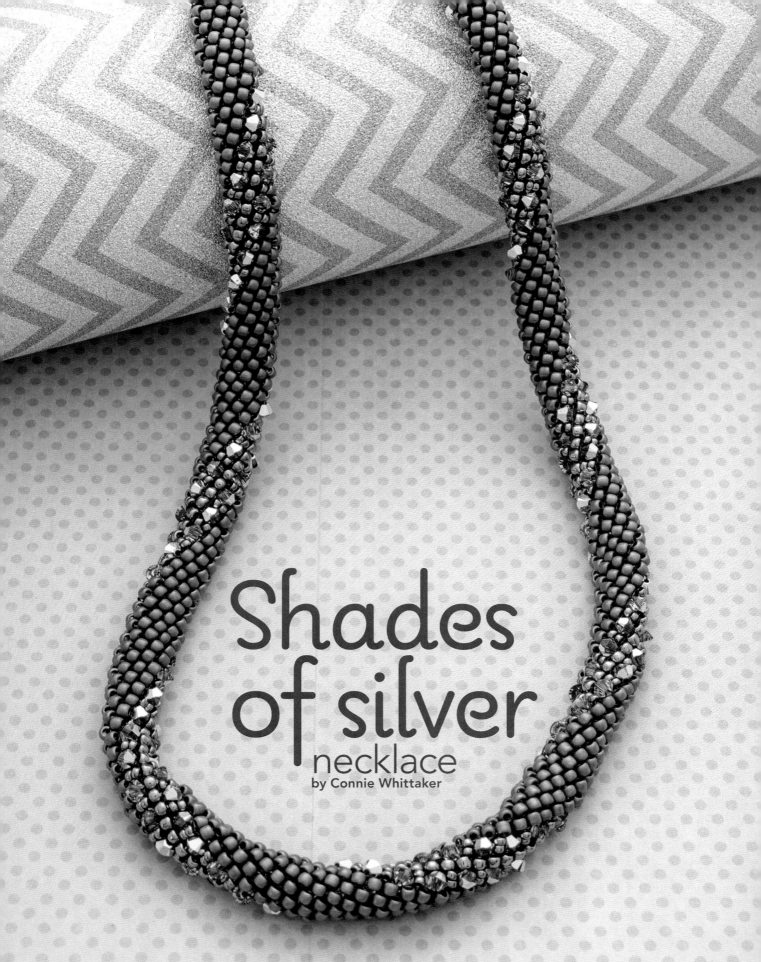

Shades of silver
necklace
by Connie Whittaker

materials

rope 19 in. (48 cm) with 3-in. (7.6 cm) extender chain

- **222** (approximately) 3 mm bicone crystals (Swarovski, crystal cal)
- 11º seed beads
  - **4 g** color A (Toho 711, nickel)
  - **20 g** color B (Toho 566, metallic silver frosted antique silver)
- **3 g** 15º seed beads (Miyuki 190, nickel plated)
- **1** lobster claw clasp
- **3 in. (7.6 cm)** small-link chain for extender
- **2** 6 mm jump rings or split rings
- Fireline, 6 lb. test
- beading needles #11 or #12
- **2** pairs of chainnose, flatnose, and/or bentnose pliers

basics

- Peytwist: single-column seam, ending
- attaching a stop bead
- ending and adding thread
- opening and closing jump rings

Sparkle this season with a Peytwist rope.

ROPE

Starter strip

1) On a comfortable length of thread, attach a stop bead, leaving a 12-in. (30 cm) tail. Starting at the upper-right corner of **figure 1**, pick up a color A 11º seed bead, a 3 mm bicone crystal, six color B 11º seed beads, two 15º seed beads, and an A. These beads will shift to form rows 1 and 2 as the next row is added. When adding the 15ºs, always pick up two 15ºs for each stitch. When sewing through them, always sew through both, treating them as one bead.

2) Work in flat even-count peyote stitch as follows to create a strip that is seven rows long:

Row 3: 1A, 3Bs, a set of 15ºs.
Row 4: 1A, 3Bs, 1 bicone.
Row 5: 1A, 3Bs, 1 bicone.
Row 6: 1A, 3Bs, a set of 15ºs.
Row 7: 1A, 3Bs, a set of 15ºs.

3) Position the tail in the upper-right corner, and work a single-column seam join **(figure 2)**. Turn the beadwork so the tail is positioned downward and the working thread is exiting the two 15ºs at the top **(photo a)**.

4) Working in single-column seam stitch, add rows as follows:

Row 8: 3Bs, 1 bicone **(photo b)**.
Row 9: 1A, 3Bs, 1 bicone **(photo c)**. Work a single-column seam turn **(photo d)**. Your thread should be exiting the bicone.

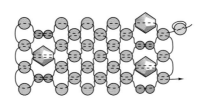

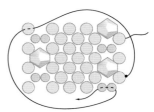

FIGURE 1   FIGURE 2

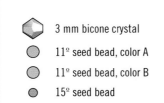

- ⬡ 3 mm bicone crystal
- ◯ 11º seed bead, color A
- ◯ 11º seed bead, color B
- ⬤ 15º seed bead

a

b

c

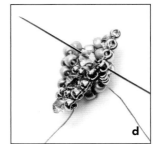

d

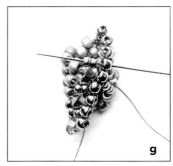

Row 10: 3Bs, a set of 15°s **(photo e)**.
Row 11: 1A, 3Bs, a set of 15°s
(photo f). Work a turn **(photo g)**.
Your thread should be exiting
the 15°s.

note You will notice that
the bicones to the left of the
As line up with the 15°s to
the right of the As, and the
15°s to the left of the As line
up with the bicones to the
right of the As.

5) Repeat step 4 for the desired
length, ending and adding thread
as needed.

Ending the rope
1) To end the rope, fill in the V
area by working six more rows following the established pattern, but
work one stitch fewer per row.
2) Sew through the up-beads at the
end of the rope to draw them into
a ring, and retrace the thread path
to tighten.

3) Pick up five As, and sew through
the opposite bead in the ring to
form a loop. Continue back through
the beads just added and the bead
your thread exited at the start of
this step, going in the same direction **(photo h)**. Retrace the thread
path through the loop, and end the
working thread.
4) Remove the stop bead from
the tail. Work as before to fill in
the V area starting with a downward row, then repeat step 3. End
the tail.

ASSEMBLY
Open a jump ring, and attach
a lobster claw clasp to the loop
on one end of the rope. Open a
jump ring, and attach the extender
chain to the loop on the other
end of the rope.

picking a clasp
If you want to be add a special pendant
to the rope occasionally, make sure the
clasp you choose will fit through a bail.

Surfin' around the waves
pendant
by Jimmie Boatright

PENDANT

1) On a comfortable length of thread, attach a stop bead, leaving an 8-in. (20 cm) tail.

2) Pick up two color A 11º cylinder beads, two color B 11º cylinder beads, two color C 11º cylinder beads, two color D 11º seed beads, two color E 11º seed beads, two color F 11º hex-cut seed beads, two color G 8º seed beads, and two color H 8º hex-cut seed beads (**figure 1, a–b**). These beads will form the first two rows as the third row is added. Do not tie any knots in these rows because you will be removing them when you join the ends together.

3) Work in flat even-count peyote stitch as follows, picking up one bead per stitch and referring to figure 1:

Row 3: H, G, F, E, D, C, B, A (**b–c**).
Row 4: A, A, B, C, D, E, F, G (**c–d**).
Row 5: G, F, E, D, C, B, A, A (**d–e**).
Row 6: A, A, A, A, B, C, D, E, F (**e–f**).
Row 7: F, E, D, C, B, A, A, A (**f–g**).
Row 8: A, A, A, A, B, C, D, E (**g–h**).
Row 9: F, E, D, C, B, A, A, A (**h–i**).
Row 10: A, A, A, B, C, D, E, F (**i–j**).
Row 11: G, F, E, D, C, B, A, A (**j–k**).
Row 12: A, A, B, C, D, E, F, G (**k–l**).
Row 13: H, G, F, E, D, C, B, A (**l–m**).
Row 14: A, B, C, D, E, F, G, H (**m–n**).
Row 15: Color I 6º seed bead, H, G, F, E, D, C, B (**n–o**).
Row 16: B, C, D, E, F, G, H, I (**o–p**). Work an increase turn: Pick up an I and an A, and sew back through the I just picked up (**p–q**). This creates a point.
Row 17: I, H, G, F, E, D, C, B (**q–r**).
Row 18: A, B, C, D, E, F, G, H (**r–s**).
Row 19: H, G, F, E, D, C, B, A (**s–t**).
Row 20: A, A, B, C, D, E, F, G (**t–u**).
Row 21: G, F, E, D, C, B, A, A (**u–v**).
Row 22: A, A, A, B, C, D, E, F (**v–w**).
Row 23: F, E, D, C, B, A, A, A (**w–x**).
Row 24: A, A, A, A, B, C, D, E (**x–y**).

4) Repeat rows 9–24 to create a total of nine "bumps" (the protruding curves) and "dips" (the concave areas between the bumps), ending with row 18 on the last repeat. End and add thread as needed.

5) Remove the stop bead, and take out the first two rows of the beadwork. Zip the two ends of the beadwork together, and end the threads.

BEZEL

1) On 4 ft. (1.2 m) of thread, pick up 30 color A cylinder beads, and sew through the first three beads again to form a ring, leaving a

materials
pendant 2¾ in (7 cm)

- **1** 12 mm rivoli (Swarovski, purple haze)
- **4 g** 6º seed beads, color I (Toho 222, dark bronze)
- **3 g** 8º hex-cut seed beads, color H (Toho SB2631, silver-lined matte amber AB; www.fusionbeads.com)
- **3 g** 8º seed beads, color G (Miyuki 454, metallic dark plum iris)
- **3 g** 11º hex-cut seed beads, color F (Miyuki 188, metallic purple gold iris)
- **3 g** 11º seed beads
  - color D (Miyuki 4218, Duracoat galvanized dusty orchid)
  - color E (Toho 704, matte Andromeda)
- 11º cylinder beads
  - **4 g** color A (Miyuki DB0611, dyed silver-lined wine)
  - **3 g** color B (Miyuki DB1843, Duracoat galvanized dark mauve)
  - **3 g** color C (Miyuki DB1831, Duracoat galvanized silver)
- **1 g** 15º seed beads (Miyuki 4201, Duracoat galvanized silver)
- Fireline, 6 lb. test
- beading needles, #11 or #12
- thread bobbin or a piece of cardboard

basics

- peyote stitch: flat even count, tubular, zipping up
- ending and adding thread
- attaching a stop bead

note Lay out your beads in order on your work surface, and label them A–I. This will help you pick up the correct beads for each stitch, alternating between ascending and descending order.

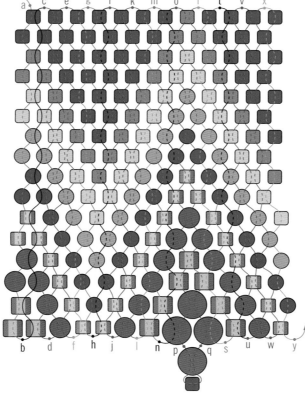

FIGURE 1

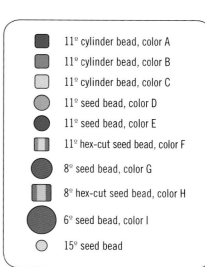

■ 11º cylinder bead, color A
■ 11º cylinder bead, color B
□ 11º cylinder bead, color C
● 11º seed bead, color D
● 11º seed bead, color E
▣ 11º hex-cut seed bead, color F
● 8º seed bead, color G
▣ 8º hex-cut seed bead, color H
● 6º seed bead, color I
○ 15º seed bead

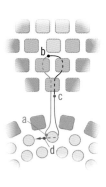

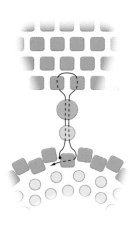

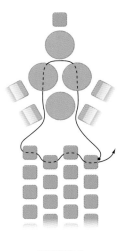

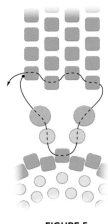

| FIGURE 2 | FIGURE 3 | FIGURE 4 | FIGURE 5 |

3-ft. (.9 m) tail. These beads will shift to form rounds 1 and 2 as the next round is added. Wrap the tail on a thread bobbin or a piece of cardboard.

2) Work rounds of tubular peyote stitch for the back of the bezel as follows, and step up at the end of each round.

Round 3: Work a round using As.

Rounds 4–5: Work both rounds using 15° seed beads.

3) Flip the beadwork over, and place the rivoli face up into the beadwork. Unwind the tail, and stitching off the As in round 1, work two rounds of 15°s for the front of the bezel, using a tight tension. End the working thread, but not the tail. With the tail, sew through the beadwork to exit the first round of 15°s added on the front of the bezel.

CENTER ATTACHMENT

You will be connecting the inside-edge cylinder beads of each bump to the front of bezel and the dips to the back of the bezel.

1) With the working thread of the bezel, sew through the edge B on the top of a bump and the next diagonal B **(figure 2, a–b)**. Turn, sew back through the adjacent B, and continue back through the first B **(b–c)**. Sew through the 15° your thread exited on the bezel, going in the same direction as before **(c–d)**, and continue through the bezel to exit the next 15° in the same round that is nearest to the following bump.

2) Work as in step 1 to attach the remaining eight bumps around the bezel, sewing through one or two 15°s in the same round so the bumps are equally spaced around the bezel. Then sew

through the bezel to the back of the pendant, exiting the last round of As nearest the 15°s.

3) With the back of the pendant facing up, pick up a D and a G, and sew through the nearest edge A near the center of the adjacent dip. Turn, and sew back through the adjacent edge A and the G and D just added, and continue through the A your thread exited at the start of the step, going in the same direction as before **(figure 3)**. Repeat this stitch to attach the remaining eight dips around the bezel, sewing through the beadwork to the nearest A in the same round of the bezel that is nearest the next dip, and end the thread.

BAIL

1) On 30 in. (.76 cm) of thread, attach a stop bead, leaving a 10-in. (25 cm) tail. Pick up four As, and work in flat even-count peyote stitch for 28 rows to form a strip. With the working thread exiting the right side of the strip, sew through a right-hand 6° on the back of the pendant, with your needle pointing toward the outside edge of the pendant. Turn, and sew back through the

adjacent 6°, with your needle pointing toward the center of the pendant. Continue through the last two rows of the strip as shown **(figure 4 and photo a)**. Retrace the thread path, and end the working thread.

2) Remove the stop bead from the tail. Sew through the nearest G and D that attach the corresponding dip to the bezel, the adjacent A in the bezel, the D and G that attach the next dip to the bezel, and the last two rows of the strip as shown **(figure 5 and photo b)**. Retrace the thread path through this connection, and end the tail.

Beautiful
butterfly pendant by Margherita Fusco

materials
blue pendant 2 in. (5 cm)

- **1** 18 x 13 mm oval crystal stone (Swarovski 4120, light turquoise)
- **5 g** 2.5 x 5 mm SuperDuo beads (pastel emerald)
- Swarovski bicone crystals
  - **14** 4 mm (white opal AB)
  - **2** 3 mm (light turquoise AB)
- **2 g** 11º seed beads (Miyuki 4201, Duracoat galvanized silver)
- **1 g** 15º seed beads (Miyuki 4201, Duracoat galvanized silver)
- **1** lobster claw clasp
- **17 in. (43 cm)** small-link chain
- **1** 8 mm jump ring
- **3** 6 mm jump rings
- Fireline, 6 lb. test
- beading needles, #12
- **2** pairs of chainnose, flat-nose, and/or bentnose pliers
- wire cutters

Find info for the alternate colorway at
FacetJewelry.com/ resourceguide

basics
- peyote stitch: tubular
- ending and adding thread
- opening and closing jump rings

FIGURE 1

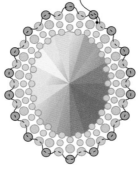

FIGURE 2

A clever combination of SuperDuos and seed beads creates a fluttering pendant that is sure to signify summer is on the way.

BUTTERFLY
Bezel
1) On a comfortable length of thread, pick up 36 11º seed beads, and sew through the first three beads again to form a ring, leaving a 6-in. (15 cm) tail. These beads will shift to form rounds 1 and 2 as the next round is added.

2) Work rounds of tubular peyote stitch for the front of the bezel as follows, and step up at the end of each round.
Round 3: Work a round using 11º s.
Rounds 4–6: Work three rounds using 15º seed beads (**figure 1**).
3) Sew through the beadwork to exit an 11º in round 1 of the outer ring. Place the oval stone facedown into the beadwork. Sewing through the 11º s in round 1, repeat rounds 3–6 to work the back of the bezel. End and add thread as needed.
4) With the bezel still facedown, sew through the beadwork to exit an 11º in the center round of 11º s on the edge (round 1). Using 11º s, work a round of "stitch-in-the-ditch" to make a base for attaching the antennae and wings (**figure 2**). Be sure to step up through the first 11º added in this round.

Antennae and wings
1) Position the bezel vertically on your work surface with the front of the bezel facing up. Sew through

the beadwork, if needed, to exit the 11º that is left of the top center bead in the round just added (**figure 3, point a**).
2) To form the antennae, pick up a 15º, nine 11º s, a 3 mm bicone crystal, and a 15º. Sew back through the 3 mm and nine 11º s. Pick up a 15º and sew through the next 11º in the previous round (**a–b**). Repeat these stitches once more to form the other antenna (**b–c**). Pick up an 11º and sew through the next 11º in the previous round (**c–d**).
3) Pick up five SuperDuos, skip the next 11º in the previous round, and sew through the following 11º (**d–e**). Using 11º s, work two peyote stitches (**e–f**). Repeat these three stitches three times, except on final repeat, work only one peyote stitch after adding the SuperDuos (**f–g**).

note Use medium tension when stitching the wings as a tight tension may make them pucker.

4) Sew through the beadwork to exit the 11º before the first set of SuperDuos (**figure 4, point a**).

note This is the perfect opportunity to retrace the thread path through the antennae, which will help stiffen them.

Legend
- 11º seed bead
- 15º seed bead
- 18 x 13 mm oval crystal
- -back surface
- 3 mm bicone crystal
- 2.5 x 5 mm SuperDuo bead
- 4 mm bicone crystal

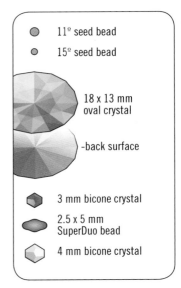

FIGURE 3

FIGURE 4

FIGURE 5

5) Pick up a 15º, and sew through the open hole of the next SuperDuo (**a–b**). Pick up a SuperDuo, and sew through the open hole of the following SuperDuo. Repeat this last stitch three times (**b–c**). Pick up a 15º, and sew through the next three 11ºs in the bezel (**c–d**). Repeat these stitches three times, except on the last repeat, sew through only two 11ºs after adding the SuperDuos (**d–e**). Sew through the beadwork to exit the first 15º picked up at the start of this step (**figure 5, point a**).

6) Pick up three 15ºs, and sew through the open hole of the next SuperDuo (**a–b**). Pick up two SuperDuos, and sew through the open hole of the following SuperDuo. Repeat this last stitch twice (**b–c**). Pick up three 15ºs, and sew through the next 15º (**c–d**).

7) Pick up two 11ºs, and sew through the next 15º (**d–e**). Pick up three 15ºs, and sew through the open hole of the following SuperDuo (**e–f**). Pick up a 4 mm bicone crystal, and sew through the open hole of the next SuperDuo. Repeat this last stitch twice (**f–g**). Pick up three 15ºs, and sew through the following 11º in the bezel (**g–h**).

8) Pick up three 15ºs, and sew through the next 11º in the round to form a small picot (**h–i**).

9) Add beads following the same pattern to create a mirror image on the opposite side of the butterfly (**i–j**). Sew through the beadwork to exit the third 15º added at the start of this round (**figure 6, point a**).

10) Pick up three 15ºs, skip the next SuperDuo, and sew through the open hole of the following SuperDuo added in the last round (**a–b**). Work five stitches using a 4 mm, a 15º, a SuperDuo, a 15º, and a 4 mm in this sequence (**b–c**).

11) Pick up three 15ºs, and sew through the next three 15ºs, two 11ºs, and three 15ºs on the adjacent wing (**c–d**).

12) Pick up three 15ºs, and sew through the next 4 mm. Repeat this stitch twice (**d–e**). Pick up four 15ºs, and sew through the next three 15ºs on this edge of the wing (**e–f**).

13) Pick up a 15ºs and sew through the center 15º of the adjacent picot (**f–g**).

14) Add beads following the same pattern to create a mirror image on the opposite side of the butterfly (**g–h**). Sew through the beadwork to exit the third 15º added at the start of this round (**figure 7, point a**).

15) Pick up three 15ºs, and sew through the next 4 mm (**a–b**). Pick up a 15º, a 4 mm, and a 15º, and sew through the open hole of the next SuperDuo in the last round (**b–c**). Pick up seven 15ºs, and sew through the SuperDuo your thread is exiting, going in the same direction to form a loop for adding the chain (**c–d**). Retrace the thread path through the loop twice (not shown in the figure for clarity). Add the same pattern of beads on the opposite side of the loop (**d–e**).

16) Sew through the beadwork to reach the wing on the other side (**e–f**), and add beads to create a mirror image on the opposite wing (**f–g**). End the thread.

ASSEMBLY

1) Cut two 8½-in. (21.6 cm) pieces of chain. Attach a 6 mm jump ring to the end link of a chain and a loop on the wing of the butterfly. Repeat this step on the opposite side of the butterfly.

2) At the end of one chain, attach an 8 mm jump ring. On the other chain, use a 6 mm jump ring to attach a lobster claw clasp.

FIGURE 6

FIGURE 7

Autumn leaves
collection   by Lane Landry

materials

all projects

- beading needles, #12
- Fireline, 6 lb. test

earrings 1 x 1¼ in. (2.5 x 3.2 cm)

- 11º seed beads
  - **1 g** color A (Toho 25C, silver-lined ruby)
  - **1 g** color B (Toho 2208, silver-lined burnt orange)
  - **2** color C (Toho 557, permanent-finish gold)
- **1** pair of earwires
- **2** 4 mm outside-diameter soldered jump rings
- **2** pairs of chainnose, bentnose, and/or flatnose pliers

bracelet 6¾ in. (17.1 cm)

- 11º seed beads
  - **3 g** color A (Toho 25C, silver-lined ruby)
  - **2 g** color B (Toho 2208, silver-lined burnt orange)
  - **7** color C (Toho 557, permanent-finish gold)
  - **2 g** color D (Toho 30B, silver-lined light orange)
- **1** 6 mm outside-diameter soldered jump ring
- **1** lobster-claw clasp

pendant 1¼ x 1½ in. (3.2 x 3.8 cm)

- 8º seed beads
  - **2 g** color A (Toho 25C, silver-lined ruby)
  - **1 g** color B (Toho 2208, silver-lined burnt orange)
  - **1 g** color D (Toho 22, silver-lined light topaz)
- **1** 11º seed bead, color C (Toho 557, permanent-finish gold)
- **1** 8 mm outside-diameter soldered jump ring

basics

- peyote stitch: flat even-count
- attaching a stop bead
- square knot
- ending thread
- opening and closing loops and jump rings

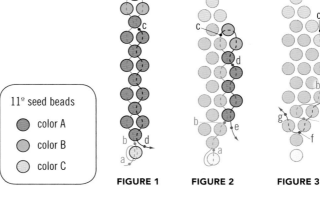

11º seed beads
- color A
- color B
- color C

FIGURE 1   FIGURE 2   FIGURE 3   FIGURE 4

EARRINGS

1) On 2 ft. (61 cm) of thread, pick up a color C 11º seed bead. Leaving a 3-in. (7.6 cm) tail, sew through the bead again to use it as a stop bead temporarily **(figure 1, a–b)**. This bead will be part of the design. Pick up nine color A 11º seed beads and three color B 11º seed beads. Sew back through the last A picked up **(b–c)**. The three Bs will form a picot at the end. Working back toward the tail, work four peyote stitches with As **(c–d)**. Pull the thread tight so the beadwork is straight. If needed, pull on the tail as well to even out the tension. Sew through the end C, and then sew back through the last two As your thread exited **(figure 2, a–b)**.

2) Work three peyote stitches with As **(b–c)**. To turn, pick up two Bs, and sew back through the last A added **(c–d)**. Work two stitches with As **(d–e)**.

3) Sew up through the adjacent A, turn, and sew back through the last A added **(figure 3, a–b)**. Make sure the thread gets tucked between the rows of As. Work two stitches with Bs **(b–c)**. To turn, pick up two Bs, and sew back through the last B added **(c–d)**. Work one stitch with a B **(d–e)**, and then sew down through the next three As **(e–f)**.

4) Sew up through the adjacent A **(f–g)**, and then work as in steps 2–3 to complete the center lobe **(figure 4)**.

5) To begin a side lobe, sew down through the next A **(figure 5, a–b)**. Pick up seven As and three Bs, and sew back through the last A just added **(b–c)**. Work three stitches with As **(c–d)**.

6) Sew through the adjacent C and back through the last two As your thread exited **(figure 6, a–b)**. Work two stitches with As **(b–c)**, turn with two Bs, and work a stitch with a B **(c–d)**.

7) Join the side lobe to the center lobe: Sew up through the adjacent A on the center lobe **(figure 7, a–b)** and the next B on the side lobe **(b–c)**. Sew down through the two adjacent As on the center lobe **(c–d)** and the next A on the side lobe **(d–e)**, and sew through the adjacent A **(e–f)**. Complete this lobe with two As and three Bs **(f–g)**.

8) To finish this side of the leaf, add a tiny lobe: Sew through the next two As **(figure 8, a–b)**. Pick up an A and four Bs, and sew back through the first B just added **(b–c)**. Join the tiny lobe to the side lobe by sewing through the adjacent A on the side lobe and the last B added on the tiny lobe **(c–d)**. Sew back through the adjacent A on the side lobe and the bottom B and A on the tiny lobe before sewing through the C **(figure 9)**.

9) Work as in steps 5–8 to add another side lobe and tiny lobe on the other side of the center lobe. At the end of step 8, do not sew through the final A and C.

10) To attach a jump ring, pick up a jump ring, and sew through the next A and then continue through the adjacent A on the opposite lobe. Sew through the jump ring again, and sew back through the A your thread just exited **(figure 10)**. Retrace the thread path through the As and jump ring. After retracing the thread path, your working thread and tail should be exiting at the same point. If they aren't, sew through the beadwork so the working thread is exiting next to the tail. Tie the working thread and tail together with a square knot, and end both threads.

11) Open the loop on an earwire, and attach it to the jump ring.

12) Repeat steps 1–11 to make another earring.

BRACELET

1) Work as in steps 1–9 of "Earrings" to make a total of seven leaf components, with the following changes:

• Start with 3 ft. (.9 m) of thread for each component, and leave a 6-in. (15 cm) tail.
• Make four components with colors A and B as in the earrings and three components substituting Bs for the As and Ds for the Bs.
• After each component is complete, sew through the beadwork to exit the tip of one side lobe, with the thread facing down toward the base of the leaf. With the tail, sew through the beadwork to exit the tip of the other side lobe, but exit with the thread facing up toward the tip of the leaf.

2) Arrange two components as shown in **figure 11**. Using the corresponding thread from each component, follow the existing thread paths to stitch the components together **(a–b and c–d)**. End each thread when the connection is secure.

3) When all the components are connected, thread a needle on the remaining thread that is facing down on an end component. Following the existing thread path, sew a lobster claw clasp to this spot **(e–f)**. Retrace the thread path, and end the thread.

4) With the remaining thread at the other end,

sew through the beadwork to exit between the side and center lobes on the end component. Following the existing thread paths, stitch a 6 mm jump ring to this spot, attaching it to the four adjacent Bs of the two lobes **(g–h)**. End the thread.

PENDANT

Following **figure 12** as a guide, work as in steps 1–9 of "Earrings" using three colors of 8º seed beads and one color C 11º. When the pendant is complete, attach a jump ring at the base of the leaf as in **figure 12**.

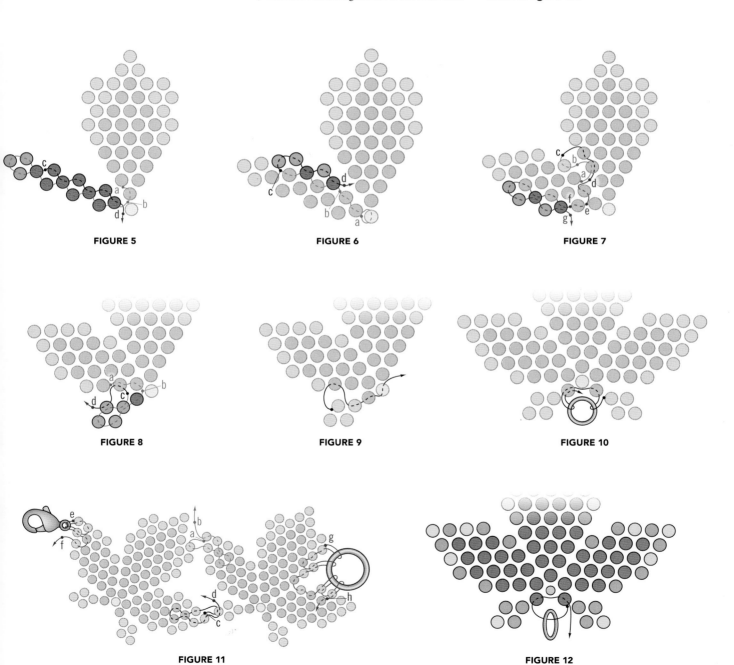

FIGURE 5

FIGURE 6

FIGURE 7

FIGURE 8

FIGURE 9

FIGURE 10

FIGURE 11

FIGURE 12

Additional stitches

LADDER STITCH

A ladder of seed beads or bugle beads is often used to begin brick stitch and herringbone stitch. To make a ladder, pick up two beads, leaving a 6-in. (15 cm) tail. Go through both beads again in the same direction. Pull the top bead down so the beads are side by side. The thread exits the bottom of the second bead (**figure 1, a–b**). Pick up a third bead, and go back through the second bead from top to bottom. Come back up the third bead (**b–c**).

Pick up a fourth bead. Go through the third bead from bottom to top and the fourth bead from top to bottom (**c–d**). Continue adding beads until you reach the desired length. To reinforce the ladder, zigzag back through it (**figure 2**).

FIGURE 1

FIGURE 2

SQUARE STITCH

1) Pick up the required number of beads for the first row. Then pick up the first bead of the second row. Go through the last bead of the first row and the first bead of the second row in the same direction as before. The new bead sits on top of the old bead, and the holes are parallel (**figure 1**).

2) Pick up the second bead of row 2, and go through the next-to-last bead of row 1. Continue through the new bead of row 2. Repeat this step for the entire row (**figure 2**).

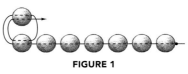

FIGURE 1

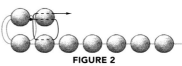

FIGURE 2

RIGHT-ANGLE WEAVE (RAW)

1) To start the first row of right-angle weave, pick up four beads, and tie them into a ring (see "Square knot"). Sew through the first three beads again (**figure 1**).

2) Pick up three beads. Sew through the last bead in the previous stitch (**figure 2, a–b**), and continue through the first two beads picked up in this stitch (**b–c**).

3) Continue adding three beads per stitch until the first row is the desired length. You are stitching in a figure-8 pattern, alternating the direction of the thread path for each stitch (**figure 3**).

Adding rows

1) To add a row, sew through the last stitch of row 1, exiting an edge bead along one side (**figure 4**).

2) Pick up three beads, and sew through the edge bead your thread exited in the previous step (**figure 5, a–b**). Continue through the first new bead (**b–c**).

3) Pick up two beads, and sew back through the next edge bead in the previous row and the bead your thread exited at the start of this step (**figure 6, a–b**). Continue through the two new beads and the following edge bead in the previous row (**b–c**).

4) Pick up two beads, and sew through the last two beads your thread exited in the previous stitch and the first new bead (**figure 7**). Continue working a figure-8 thread path, picking up two beads per stitch for the rest of the row.

FIGURE 1

FIGURE 2

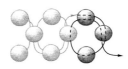

FIGURE 3

FIGURE 4

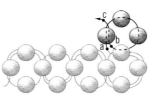

FIGURE 5

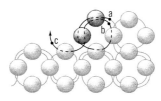

FIGURE 6

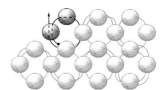

FIGURE 7

HERRINGBONE STITCH

Start with an even number of beads stitched into a ladder (see Ladder). Turn the ladder, if necessary, so your thread exits the end bead pointing up.

Pick up two beads, and go down through the next bead on the ladder (figure 1, a–b). Come up through the third bead on the ladder, pick up two beads, and go down through the fourth bead (b–c). Repeat across the ladder.

To turn, come back up through the second-to-last bead, and continue through the last bead added in the previous row (figure 2, a–b). Pick up two beads, go down through the next bead in that row, and come up through the next bead (b–c). Repeat across the row.

FIGURE 1

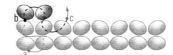

FIGURE 2

CUBIC RIGHT-ANGLE WEAVE (CRAW)

Making the first CRAW unit

1) On the specified length of thread, pick up four beads. Tie the beads into a ring with a square knot, leaving the specified length tail, and continue through the first two beads in the ring. This ring of beads will count as the first stitch of the unit.

2) Work two right-angle weave stitches off of the bead your thread is exiting to create a flat strip of right-angle weave.

3) To join the first and last stitches: Pick up a bead, sew through the end bead in the first stitch (figure 1, a–b), pick up a bead, and sew through the end bead in the last stitch (b–c). A three-dimensional view of the resulting cube-shaped unit is shown in (figure 2).

4) To make the unit more stable, sew through the four beads at the top of the unit (figure 3). Sew through the beadwork to the bottom of the unit, and sew through the four remaining beads. This completes the first CRAW unit.

Making more CRAW units

1) Each new CRAW unit is worked off of the top four beads of the previous unit (figure 4). Sew through the beadwork to exit one of these top beads.

2) For the first stitch of the new unit: Pick up three beads, and sew through the top bead your thread exited at the start of this step. Continue through the three beads just picked up (photo a). Sew through the next top bead in the previous unit.

3) For the second stitch of the new unit: Pick up two beads, and sew through the side bead in the previous stitch, the top bead your thread exited at the start of this stitch (photo b), and the next top bead in the previous unit.

4) For the third stitch of the new unit: Repeat step 3 (photo c), and continue through the side bead in the first stitch of the new unit.

5) For the fourth stitch of the new unit: Pick up a bead, and sew through the side bead in the previous stitch and the top bead in the previous unit (photo d).

6) To make the unit more stable, sew through the beadwork to exit a top bead in the new unit, and sew through all four top beads (photo e). This completes the new CRAW unit.

7) Repeat steps 2–6 for the desired number of CRAW units.

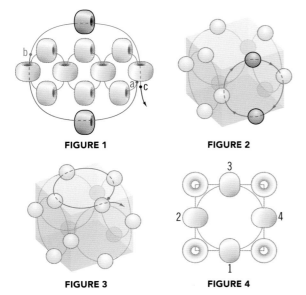

FIGURE 1   **FIGURE 2**

FIGURE 3   **FIGURE 4**

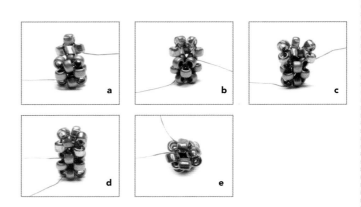

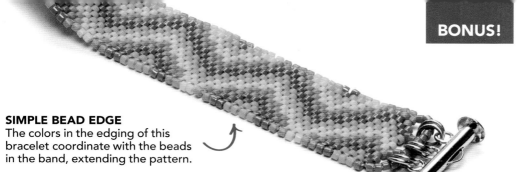

SIMPLE BEAD EDGE
The colors in the edging of this bracelet coordinate with the beads in the band, extending the pattern.

FIGURE 1

POINTED EDGE
The point on this edge change color to match the color of the beads below.

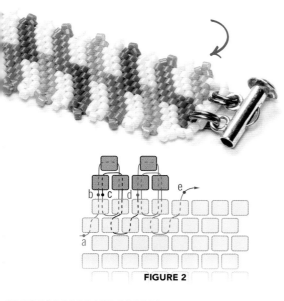

FIGURE 2

SIDE PETAL EDGE
This bracelet alternates a side petal edge with two pointed edge picots.

FIGURE 3

Edging techniques

techniques by Jamie Cloud Eakin

Many popular beading techniques, including peyote stitch, end up with exposed bead holes and thread on the edge. Some people like this look, while others simply accept it as a result of the technique. But many beaders find this unacceptable in their beadwork. If you're among this group, take heart — you're not alone and the good news is that there are several ways to cover this edge.

SIMPLE BEAD EDGE

This technique provides the simplest solution. It is easy to stitch and hides the bead holes and exposed thread. You can use one color to provide a frame for your beadwork or change colors to blend with or otherwise complement the colors in your piece.

1) Sew up through two edge beads at the end (figure 1, **a–b**).
2) Pick up an embellishment bead, and sew through the adjacent three beads so that your thread comes back out through the second edge bead (**b–c**). Repeat this stitch along the entire edge (**c–d**). Sew through to the other edge, and repeat.

POINTED EDGE
(AKA PICOT EDGE)

There are more beads added to the edge in this technique, which increases the overall width of the beadwork more than the simple bead edge. This also gives you more opportunities to create your own design using different colors or bead sizes.

1) Sew up through two edge beads in row 1 (figure 2, **a–b**).
2) Pick up three embellishment beads, and sew down through the edge bead in the next row and up through the edge bead in the previous row (**b–c**). Sew through the first and third beads just added, down through the two edge beads in the

next row and up through the corresponding two beads in the following row (**c–d**).
3) Repeat step 2 (**d–e**) along the entire edge. Sew through to the other edge, and repeat.

SIDE PETAL EDGE

This edge is easy, fast, and adds more pizzazz to the beadwork that the other two techniques. The technique involves using a center bead surrounded by smaller beads to create a rounded profile. The edge beads are usually added over a base of four beads, but you can change the base count if desired to create a taller loop (skip fewer edge beads) or one that hugs the edge closer (skip more edge beads). Use 3 mm beads, such as round, oval, or bicone, for the center bead. This is a great technique to use if you want to bling up a seed bead bracelet with some crystals.

1) Sew up through two edge beads in row 1 (figure 3, **a–b**).
2) Pick up a 15º seed bead, an 11º seed bead, a 3 mm bead, an 11º, and a 15º. Skip two edge beads, and sew through the top two or three edge beads in the next row and the corresponding beads in the following row (**b–c**).
3) Repeat step 2 (**c–d**) along the entire edge. Reinforce by stitching through the entire row of edging again, except this time sew down and up through only one bead along the edge.
4) Sew through the beadwork to exit the other edge, and repeat.

Contributors

Jimmie Boatright is a retired public school educator who teaches her original designs at Beadjoux Bead Shop in Braselton, Georgia. Visit www.beadjoux.com to see more of her designs or to purchase patterns.

Contact **Antonio Calles** in care of Kalmbach Books.

Jamie Cloud Eakin is the author of *Beading with Cabochons* and *Bead Embroidery Jewelry Projects* (Lark), and her designs appear in other Lark books including *Beading with World Beads* by Ray Hemachandra and *Beading All Stars*. Her beaded creations are sold in fine galleries. She lives in Modesto, CA. Visit studiojamie.com for more information.

Lorraine Coetzee of Cape Town, South Africa, has been beading for about six years. She sells jewelry and patterns on the Internet. To see more of her work, visit www.facebook.com/TrinityDesignerJewelry.

Jane Danley Cruz is the author of *Ready, Set, Bead!* and is a former associate editor for *Bead&Button* magazine. She currently lives in Illinois with her husband and daughter. Contact her via e-mail at jmdcruz262@gmail.com.

Magdalena Dec is from Warsaw, Poland. Beading is her passion, and she likes to make custom jewelry for clients. See her work at www.etsy.com/shop/ErganeBeading.

Diane Fitzgerald is an internationally recognized bead artist, teacher, and author. Of her twelve books, Diane's most recent is *The Joy of Two-Hole Beads*, and recently her 150th article was published in *Bead&Button* magazine. She is perhaps most well known for her classic Ginkgo Leaf Necklace. Visit her website, dianefitzgerald.com.

Margherita Fusco lives in the north of Italy and loves to create handmade jewels (peyote, crochet, brick stitch, and so on). See more of her work at www.etsy.com/shop/75marghe75.

Julia Gerlach is the former Editor of *Bead&Button* magazine. Contact her in care of Kalmbach Books.

Ellie Hamlett is an enthusiastic beader and creator of patterns. She enjoys designing with a variety of shaped and multi-hole beads. She can be contacted via thebuffalobeadgallery@gmail.com. Her patterns and kits are available at thebuffalobeadgallery.com.

Diane Jolie is Senior Associate Editor of *Bead&Button* magazine. Contact her in care of Kalmbach Books.

Lisa Kan is a beader and lampwork artist who enjoys incorporating innovative components and seed beads in designing distinctively elegant beadwork with a vintage feel. She draws her inspiration from nature, history, ceramics, Japanese arts and aesthetics, and Victorian-era jewelry, and is the author of *Bead Romantique: Elegant Beadweaving Designs*. Contact Lisa through her website, lisakan.com.

Michele Klous lives in Connecticut. She recently became a member of The BeadSmith Inspiration Squad. Visit her her shop, Many Stitches, on Facebook, or see more of her work at www.etsy.com/shop/ManyStitchesInTime.

Lane Landry and her daughter Cara are self-employed artists who create detailed beading tutorials available on SimpleBeadPatterns.com and SimpleBeadPatterns.Etsy.com. When not beading, Lane shares her love of painting on Twitch.tv/PaintHappy.

Gerlinde Lenz teaches beadweaving and has developed many unique stitches, including peyote with a twist (Peytwist). Visit her Facebook page for more information, or join her "Peyote with a Twist—Not Crochet" Facebook group.

Graziella Malara is an artisan from Pomezia, Italy, who is in love with the beadweaving technique. Visit her Etsy shop, www.etsy.com/shop/GraziellaMalara.

June Malone is a full-time bead artist in New Mexico who creates custom designs and one-of-a-kind pieces to sell at art festivals. She has been a featured artist in *Bead&Button* and *Beadwork* magazines, and is a member of Beadsmith's Inspiration Squad. Her kits are sold in her Etsy shop (Enchanted Beads by JM), and she teaches beaders of all skill levels. She is active on Facebook and can be reached by email at beader@cableone.net. To see some of her designs and learn more, visit her website, www.enchantedbeader.com.

Regina Payne says designing and creating beaded jewelry is her passion. She has been creating for 29 years and has been published in *Beadwork* magazine, *Perlen Poesie*, *Bead&Button*, and *Jewelry Crafts*. Visit her website, nightowlstudiojewels.com, to view more of her work.

Theodora Seimeni is a full-time jewelry designer from Greece. She loves to combine different techniques and materials such as seed beads, cylinder beads, and crystals to create unique pieces that feature clean lines. Her tutorials aim to help beading friends of all skill levels to complete advanced projects. See more of her work at zialolabeadsit.etsy.com and https://zialolabeadsit.indiemade.com/store.

Connie Whittaker is Senior Technical Editor of *Bead&Button* magazine. Contact her at cwhittaker@beadandbutton.com.

Kristy Zgoda has been drawing, painting, sculpting ever since she can remember—especially animals. See her work at www.etsy.com/shop/Kristyz.

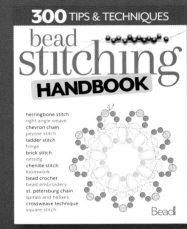